Sam Elkin has a sharp eye and a wit that crackles. *Detachable Penis* is searching in its honesty and possesses a streetwise kindness. Elkin makes us feel as if we, too, are at the shoreline of an old life, contemplating the wide expanse of the one to begin. He knows that the body of the law and the human body are similar. They contain so much; they contain us. Here, Elkin creates a new body of work that grapples with both and never settles for the narrow wisdoms of the past.
Rick Morton

There is a quiet audacity to Sam's story and his writing that is reminiscent of how LGBTQIA+ people have had to live their lives for so long. The beefy tales in *Detachable Penis* are at once enraging, funny and hopeful – the hallmarks of good storytelling. I am thrilled that Sam is helping to carve out a shiny new space in Australian letters. The work sits boldly and imaginatively on the queer horizon.
George Haddad

Detachable Penis is a thoroughly contemporary and deeply heartfelt book. It is a layered, compelling text: at once the diary of a community lawyer working with a case-load to make your head spin, advising and representing clients who have almost invariably been failed by our society, and it is a frank, politically-astute, and very funny account of his own queer life and transition. What I loved most about this excellent book is how it demonstrates the simultaneity of crisis and liberation for queer people; there is so much power working against queer liberation, but queer liberation cannot in fact be suppressed.

I read this book up late, one sitting, eyes glued to the page. It's fantastic! And yes, there is a detachable, crocheted penis in there.
Ellena Savage

I loved this book. At once a unique insight into the trials and tribulations of an LGBTIQ legal service, and an intimate journal of Elkin's gender transition, it breaks new ground in the growing genre of trans memoirs. It's fascinating, funny, steadfast and sometimes angry, vulnerable, brave and honest. Elkin writes with a keen sense of place and character, mapping territory rarely seen before about surgical and medical options currently available to transmen in Australia, revealing and interrogating as much about our society as he does about himself. Elkin's moral compass never falters, but he is never didactic nor prescriptive. He is alert to both the big machinery of political systems and the little details of everyday interactions with people. The personal nature of the book feels like a gift; it is never cloying, sentimental nor indulgent. Grab a copy of Sam Elkin's *Detachable Penis*. And read it now.
Fiona Kelly McGregor

In this darkly funny tale of community law and gender transition, Sam Elkin lifts the lid on the shiny queer rainbow to reveal the dysfunction and lateral violence that lie beneath. A born storyteller, with a knack for finding the absurdity in the darkest situations, Elkin gives us a penetrating portrait of contemporary queer and trans politics, in all their contradictions and complexity. Riveting, refreshingly honest and wonderfully humane, *Detachable Penis* is a triumphant debut that refuses the easy comforts of a party line.
Yves Rees

A work of great heart and brain. Elkin is compulsory reading, always.
Chloe Hooper

DETACHABLE PENIS

Sam Elkin

Sam Elkin is a writer, lawyer and co-editor of *Nothing to Hide: Voices of Trans and Gender Diverse Australia* (Allen & Unwin, 2022). Born in England and raised on Noongar land, Sam now lives on unceded Wurundjeri land. Sam's essays have been published in *Griffith Review*, *Australian Book Review*, *Sydney Review of Books* and *Kill Your Darlings*. He hosts the 3RRR radio show Queer View Mirror and is a tilde Melbourne Trans & Gender-Diverse Film Festival board member. *Detachable Penis: A Queer Legal Saga* is his first book.

DETACHABLE
PENIS

A Queer Legal Saga

Sam Elkin

WILFRID LAURIER
UNIVERSITY PRESS

Wilfrid Laurier University Press acknowledges the support of the Canada Council for the Arts for our publishing program. We acknowledge the financial support of the Government of Canada through the Canada Book Fund for our publishing activities. Funding provided by the Government of Ontario and the Ontario Arts Council. This work was supported by the Research Support Fund.

Library and Archives Canada Cataloguing in Publication

Title: Detachable penis : a queer legal saga / Sam Elkin.
Names: Elkin, Sam (Lawyer), author
Identifiers: Canadiana (print) 20240338367 | Canadiana (ebook) 20240338510 | ISBN 9781771126656 (softcover) | ISBN 9781771126663 (EPUB) | ISBN 9781771126670 (PDF)
Subjects: LCSH: Elkin, Sam (Lawyer) | LCSH: Transgender people—Civil rights—Australia. | LCSH: Gay rights—Australia. | LCSH: Transgender people—Legal status, laws, etc.—Australia. | LCSH: Gay people—Legal status, laws, etc.—Australia. | LCSH: Transgender people—Australia—Identity. | LCSH: Lawyers—Australia—Biography. | LCSH: Transgender men—Australia—Biography. | LCGFT: Autobiographies.
Classification: LCC HQ77.95.A8 E45 2024 | DDC 323.3/270994—dc23

Cover design by Aldo Fierro. Interior design by Lasertype. Front cover image: Stuffed crochet cock, Brett Walker, Bretty Bobetty Art.

Published and distributed in North America by Wilfrid Laurier University Press, 75 University Avenue West, Waterloo, ON N2L 3C5, Canada www.wlupress.wlu.ca/

Published and distributed outside North America by Upswell Publishing, 8 Myrtle Street, Perth, WA, 6000, Australia https://upswellpublishing.com

This book is printed on FSC® certified paper. It contains recycled materials and other controlled sources, is processed chlorine-free, and is manufactured using biogas energy.
Printed in Canada

Dedicated to the little gay kids of Werribee

The events in this book took place on the vast, unceded lands of the Wurundjeri Woi Wurrung, Boon Wurrung, Brataualung, Noongar, Turrbal, Jagera and Kabi Kabi peoples. This book was written on those lands, as well as on Gundungurra, Darug and Taungurung Country.

Author's Note

This is a work of narrative non-fiction. In some cases, the names of individuals and organisations have been changed to protect their privacy. All client names, identifying features and incidental information have been significantly altered to protect confidentiality. Some events have been amalgamated or compressed, and dialogue has been re-created based on the author's best recollections.

"We're forced to walk a difficult line by this insistence that we only write about our personal journeys," I told the audience. "We end up in this position of only being allowed to represent ourselves, but having to make sure we don't misrepresent everyone. This creates some division in our communities – everyone has their own opinion about what's good representation and what isn't, and you can't please them all."

Juliet Jacques, **Trans: A Memoir**

In a society that rewards the possessor of the penis with obvious political, economic, and cultural benefits, women would have to be a little obtuse not to envy it; they would have to be a little obtuse not to want the social advantages that automatically accrue to the possessor of the penis, particularly if he happens to be white.

Mari Ruti, **Penis Envy and Other Bad Feelings: The Emotional Costs of Everyday Life**

Is this story tragic? Or fit for laughter?
Do we ever learn from the things we do?
Sweethearts, god, I wish I knew.

Cat Fitzpatrick, **The Call-Out: A Novel in Rhyme**

Contents

Chapter 1
Queer Legal Service

Back then, I hadn't known much about St Kilda other than what I'd absorbed from watching episodes of *The Secret Life of Us*. In my mind, St Kilda was a gritty seaside suburb full of decaying art deco apartments, dingy bars and heroin users. When I got off the train for my first day of work and took in the eclectic mix of rich, trendy young mums, black-clad Hasidic Jewish men with long, swirling curls, stylish coffee shops and late-model Mercedes crawling down Carlisle Street, I thought I'd come to the wrong place.

I saw the small, dilapidated sign for my new workplace on the corner of Chapel Street. Stuffed inside a nineteenth-century triangular brown brick schoolhouse, St Kilda Legal Service was operating in the literal shadows of the tall, run-down red-and-cream Gothic brick church next door. Its imposing white cross, which sat atop a 30-metre turret, made me wonder if this was perhaps not in fact the ideal location for Victoria's inaugural queer legal service. But I wasn't here to be picky. I was here to embrace my destiny.

At 8.59 a.m., with a takeaway coffee in hand, I knocked on the still-shuttered front door. When no one answered, I started worrying if I'd got the day wrong. I knocked a couple more times before a dour-looking middle-aged man in a fleece jumper opened the door a crack, eyeing me suspiciously through a heavy-duty chain latch.

'Food bank doesn't open until 9.30,' he said.

'I'm actually starting work here today,' I replied.

He looked at me blankly.

'As a lawyer?' I said, hoping this might clear things up.

He promptly shut the door in my face.

Bewildered, I was struggling to think of what to do next when the man noisily unbolted the chain and the door swung open.

'Come in quickly, then. I can't leave the door open otherwise everyone will start streaming in,' he said.

As I crossed the threshold, I felt as though I'd stepped through a portal to the past. I was back with Mum in the waiting room of the Mirrabooka public housing authority in outer suburban Perth. Here at St Kilda Community Centre, colourful flyers for family violence services and homelessness support spilled out of a metal rack affixed to the wall. A well-used children's toy box was crammed into the corner of the tiny waiting room, which fit three snugly placed metal chairs.

The man pointed towards an internal frosted glass door.

'I'm just the front desk volunteer for the food service. Legal sits in there. You got a key?' he asked.

I shook my head.

'Well, I can't let you in because I don't know who you are. You'll have to wait here until one of them arrives.'

I sat down on a banged-up metal chair and stared at the shiny toy cars on a tiny felt racetrack. My first-day excitement was depleting fast. By 9.20 a.m., a small group of rough sleepers had amassed out the front, smoking and idly chatting. I presumed they were here for the pre-prepared meal relief boxes, full of canned corn and beets, loaves of white sliced bread and a few bruised apples. A handwritten sign above the counter read, 'Yes we have nappies, one box per day max'.

* * *

When I'd seen that St Kilda Legal Service had received a grant to run a two-year queer legal service pilot and were looking for an experienced social justice lawyer, it seemed like the dream job for me. I'd be able to marry my passion for community law with my love of LGBTIQ culture. Another bonus would be getting to explore a whole new part of Melbourne, my adopted home. I wasn't surprised that an initiative like this had finally been funded. Same-sex marriage had just been passed following 2017's national postal survey, and a lot of people were feeling guilty about the ugly public debate that the queer community had been subjected to.

On the day of my job interview, I'd chosen the same outfit I'd worn for years for any formal occasion: a small black women's suit that I hoped looked unisex, an ironed checked shirt and a pair of brown brogues. I looked just like one of the many soft butch, bespectacled lesbians who bounced around Melbourne's social justice sector on modest, fixed-term contracts. But I wasn't. I was the latest recruit in the butch to trans masc pipeline, having been on a one-quarter dose of testosterone for exactly one week.

I was interviewed by Polina, the youngish principal lawyer, and the middle-aged, balding board chair. The unairconditioned meeting room in the ramshackle community centre was stifling in the February afternoon heat. I'd responded to their interview questions with my experiences fighting tenancy evictions in tribunals in Sydney, making bail applications for family violence perpetrators in the Morwell police lock-up, and running Centrelink appeals for Larrakia long grass clients in Darwin.

'And can you tell us about your prior experience with the GLTBI community?'

The board chair stumbled over this acronym in such a way that I was certain he'd never had cause to say it out loud before.

I smiled and gave highlights from my time at La Trobe University working as a queer officer, running student network meetings in the campus 'Rainbow Room', and volunteering with Joy 94.9, Melbourne's queer radio station.

This moment would have absolutely been the time to disclose to my prospective new employers about my intended change in hormonal status. But I didn't know how to bring it up. And I really wanted this job. Something about these two made me think that disclosing my trans status would make me look complicated. So, I merely confirmed in closing that I was a proud member of the LGBTIQ community, without specifying which bit.

A week later, Polina offered me a contract. Only then did I waver. I'd be giving up a cushy permanent Legal Aid job with great colleagues for a fixed-term role on lower pay that would always be of uncertain funding. But Legal Aid was also huge. The thought of transitioning in front of hundreds of colleagues, spread out across four open-plan office floors, did not appeal. At least there were only half a dozen people to come out to here at St Kilda Legal Service. So, I took the job.

Polina finally walked through the door, puffing slightly in a reflective silver cycling jacket.

'Sorry, Sam, traffic was terrible. Welcome!'

She gave me an awkward shoulder pat and took me through to the legal service. It was a low-ceilinged, wood-panelled workplace, full of cheap furniture, outdated lawbooks and overflowing beige filing cabinets. I'd worked in some humble offices over the years, but this place took the cake. Polina explained that the legal service was co-located within St Kilda Community Centre, an organisation staffed by social workers and financial counsellors, and that only six desks in the left-hand corridor 'belonged' to us.

I followed Polina into her cramped, galley-style office. I had to move a few thick red client files off her spare chair to sit down. Polina gave me a quick spiel about St Kilda Legal Service's history offering free legal support to the homeless, the street-based sex workers and the drug users who had given the area its 'colourful' reputation. I nodded enthusiastically. This was exactly the kind of impactful work I wanted to do.

She handed me the centre's annual report, its risk management guide and the successful grant application that its drug outreach lawyer, Henry, had written to get the funding for my job.

'Henry is really the expert on all this. I've only been here a few months myself. He's at the Salvation Army food kitchen doing a fines clinic right now, but I'm sure you'll see him later.'

The sound of someone shuffling in via the back door interrupted our discussion. It was an older woman, her dyed blonde hair and transition lenses reminding me of the friendly, knockabout women who'd run my primary-school canteen in the outer northern Perth suburb of Marangaroo.

'Sandie, you're here,' said Polina. 'Come and meet Sam. Sandie is St Kilda Legal Service's very longstanding administrative assistant. How long have you been working here now, Sandie?' Polina asked.

'I've been here since the day it opened in 1973,' Sandie said with a grin, the smell of cigarette smoke wafting towards us as she spoke.

'Well, your timing's perfect. I've just got to duck off to a network meeting. Sandie, can you find Sam a desk and a laptop?' Polina asked, as she pulled her cycling jacket back on.

After Polina left, I skimmed through the amateurishly formatted annual report, full of stock images of Luna Park's grinning clown face and St Kilda's famous Acland Street cake shops, while Sandie tried in vain to find me the spare laptop.

'I swear I locked it in here the other day,' she said, pointing to one of many tiny cupboards in her overflowing work pod.

I reassured her that I was not in any hurry to begin work and wandered into the kitchen to make myself a tea. I found a passably clean vintage mug commemorating Kevin Rudd's 2008 National Apology to the Stolen Generations and put the kettle on.

As my tea brewed, I perused a pin-up board full of ageing newspaper clippings about homelessness prevention and drug support initiatives alongside a weathered Leunig cartoon. There were handwritten notes of varying levels of politeness imploring staff to do their own dishes and to remember to set the building alarm at the end of the day.

I then read the grant application for a queer legal service to tackle 'the effects of entrenched stigma and discrimination by addressing the unmet legal needs of the queer community'. This grant would pay my wages and be my operating guide for the next two years.

The key deliverables section included an eye-watering amount of work. We'd promised to assist hundreds of LGBTIQ clients during the pilot project in any area of legal need that they presented with, run training and professional development sessions, promote the service at universities and in community media and, finally, to end the project with a detailed report of what we'd learnt.

My mission over the next two years was to:

- run a health justice partnership based at Pink Panther, a Melbourne LGBTIQ health organisation

- deliver a minimum of 500 legal advices and run 250 individual cases

- provide five legal education sessions to the community

- create an LGBTIQ inclusive practice toolkit for lawyers for national distribution

- write a comprehensive report summarising unmet legal needs across the LGBTIQ community.

How was I meant to do all this on my own? I suddenly felt a deep yearning for my supportive team of colleagues back at Legal Aid. As I began to take in the immensity of the task before me, my concentration was broken by the wet, whooshing sound of the office's sole toilet flushing noisily next door. It sounded like a plane coming into land. When I went into the toilet a few minutes later, I was alarmed to see a series of green and red lights blinking at me from a corner of the room. Was it a hidden camera? I went to investigate. The lights were emanating from a large metallic box, which was hot to touch. It was an ancient but still entirely operational desktop computer. In the toilet. Could it be possible that they sometimes crammed the staff into the actual toilet? Would I be expected to hot desk from the toilet if Sandie couldn't find me a laptop?

When I went to enquire about the status of my laptop, I asked about the toilet PC.

'Oh, that's the server. It overheats and turns itself off if we put it anywhere else,' Sandie said.

When she informed me that she still had not located the laptop, I decided to take myself out for an early lunch. I passed the surly front desk volunteer on my way out.

'Someone told me you're the new GLBT lawyer,' he said.

Why are the G's always back in front around here? I thought to myself.

'That's me,' I replied.

'Well, I don't think it's right,' the man said, shaking his head.

'Erm, in what way?'

'I don't see why gays or lesbians need special privileges. Everyone should be treated equally. That's what I think,' he said.

In response, I recited almost word for word what Henry had written in the grant application. I mentioned the community's historical distrust of the police, stemming from the history of homosexuality being criminalised and the impact of the AIDS crisis on older people's physical and emotional health. He was not convinced.

'Yeah, well, I just don't think it's right,' he repeated flatly.

God, if he didn't like gays and lesbians, he was going to like me even less when I started sprouting a moustache.

I went into a hip-looking bagel shop on Chapel Street to try to shake off the bad interaction. I sat down at an outside table in the afternoon sun. Then I realised I was sitting directly across the road from St Kilda Police Station, as two uniformed officers in their navy and hi-vis stepped out of their building towards the coffee shop next door. I felt blindsided and demoralised. This day was not going at all how I'd imagined.

As I was staring off into space, a rotund, bearded man with glasses tapped me on the shoulder.

'Sam? I'm Henry,' he said.

His backpack, spilling open with client paperwork, thudded as Henry dumped it down on a spare chair and took a seat opposite.

'Congratulations on the new job,' he said.

Henry and I chatted about community law gossip: which centres had amalgamated recently or lost their funding, how bad the new Fines Victoria system was, and the latest drama with our dysfunctional peak body. I liked Henry immediately. I asked him how he found working at St Kilda Legal Service.

'Look, I'm not going to lie. This place is a bit nuts right now. The volunteers hate the paid staff, the board hates Polina, and Legal Aid has threatened to defund us if Polina doesn't ram through all these new accountability measures. Sandie's lovely, but I'm pretty sure she doesn't know how to use a computer. But you'll be fine since you'll be over at Pink Panther most of the time,' he said.

We sat chatting over bagels and coffee, and then Henry took me on a quick tour of the local support services on Grey Street.

'Here's the Salvation Army needle exchange and Sacred Heart Mission,' he said, pointing out more red-and-tan brick buildings. 'There's also a rehab service called Windana and a sex worker organisation called RhED down that way,' Henry said, as we wandered through the St Kilda streets.

As we headed back towards our office, he pointed at a line of disadvantaged-looking people snaking around the street.

'That's the food kitchen, which should be opening its doors . . . nowish,' he said, checking the time on his cracked phone. 'That's where I do another fines clinic a couple of days a week.'

I couldn't believe how much work Henry seemed to be doing.

'Do you like working here?' I asked.

Henry laughed.

'Well, let's just say I'm actively looking for other work,' he said.

A creeping worry suddenly came over me. Had I swanned in and taken the job that Henry had wanted? Had he gone above and beyond by trying to get money for a new role that he'd like to do, only for Polina to give it away to someone else? That sounded like exactly the kind of fuckery that always seemed to happen in this industry.

When we got back, Sandie had found me an ancient Dell laptop and an even older Motorola flip phone.

'We get less and less funding every year, so we just have to make do with what we've got,' Sandie said with a sigh. I thanked her and decided to make my way over to Pink Panther to see where I'd be spending most of my time. I desperately hoped that things would be less chaotic over there.

* * *

I got the tram down Chapel Street, heading for Pink Panther's schmick headquarters on St Kilda Road. I'd always thought of these wide streets as the most soulless part of Melbourne, with its unending array of glass and steel tower blocks. As I gazed out of the tram window, I was reminded of the true crime podcast I'd just listened to about the terrible death of Phoebe Handsjuk, who was killed in 2010 when she plunged to her death in the garbage chute of one of these luxury high-rise apartment buildings. It was a 40-metre fall from the chute's entry hatch on the twelfth floor. She'd managed to survive the fall but bled to death in the dark after her foot was severed by the garbage compactor. Her partner at the time, a son of a retired Supreme Court judge, was the prime suspect. The coroner had found, seemingly incredulously, that she'd got into the chute herself while sleepwalking under the influence of alcohol and prescription medication. The whole thing gave me a sick feeling that the old boys club was covering up what had happened to protect one of their own. It reinforced my sense that things were far from fair in the justice system.

When I arrived at Pink Panther's chrome and glass offices, a tall, fashionable concierge smiled at me as she gave me a visitor pass and directed me up to level six.

When I stepped into the elevator, my eyes were buffeted by gigantic rainbow poster art that read, 'You Are Loved' and 'All Sexualities, Genders, Identities and Cultures Welcome Here'. As my brogues clicked on the polished concrete in Pink Panther's reception, I noticed a large, colourful bowl of condoms and lube on the glass table in the waiting area. A life-size poster of a buff man in Y-fronts stood by the reception desk, spruiking the benefits of regular STI testing.

A svelte, diminutive receptionist called Bao, who stood beside the scantily clad printed man, squealed and gave me a kiss on both cheeks.

'Sam, we are so excited to meet you. Wow, a real lawyer, here to help us all! Come in, come in.'

I followed Bao as he sashayed through to the expansive offices behind reception. He showed me to my desk, which had an up-to-the minute monitor and docking station.

He then took me on a tour, where I was greeted warmly by a fresh-faced team of clinical psychologists, drug and alcohol counsellors and family violence support staff.

'We can't wait to work with you. We know so many people who could benefit from your support,' said one of the counsellors.

I smiled and nodded at everyone, wondering how on earth I was going to remember all their names. Bao then answered my unstated question by showing me a bright wall of staff polaroid photos. Under-neath each image, the name, position and pronouns of each staff member was prominently displayed. At least five staff used they/them pronouns.

'Okay, photo time!' said Bao, as he lined me up against the wall.

I stood awkwardly, like a tin soldier, projecting the exact opposite of Bao's camp fabulousness.

'What pronouns do you use?' he asked, as we both watched the image of an uncertain-looking, short butch with black-rimmed glasses begin to appear in the polaroid.

'Um … they/them?' I said, almost as a question.

I'd never actually had the nerve to use gender-neutral pronouns in the workplace before.

'Yaaas! We love gender diversity here,' said Bao, as he wrote my pronouns beneath my name.

We finished the tour at the toilets. 'These ones on your left have urinals and the ones on your right have sanitary bins in every stall, but they are all gender-neutral, so please use whichever space you feel most comfortable in,' he said with a smile.

Bao then handed me a rainbow lanyard. 'Let me know if you need anything, lovely, anything at all.'

What a sweet workplace, I thought. Even if St Kilda Legal Service was a bit iffy, it seemed like I'd be welcome here at Pink Panther. Maybe this was going to work out after all.

Chapter 2
The Genderbread Man

As the counsellor predicted, many clients of Pink Panther were in legal trouble.

My first client was Tommy, a blonde 28-year-old from South Yarra wearing a tight ruby t-shirt and Gucci denim jeans. He kept his Ray Bans on as he presented me with a crumpled summons to attend the Magistrates Court in a fortnight.

I flicked through his court documents as we sat together in an interview room. He'd been charged with breaching an intervention order, smashing the headlights of his ex-boyfriend's Jeep Wrangler and possessing GHB, meth and cannabis.

'Have you got any prior convictions, Tommy?' I asked.

He shook his head. 'I've never been in any trouble. This has just been, like, a really shitty time. You know he hooked up with my housemate?'

I offered Tommy a non-committal nod as I peered at the referral notes from Hugo, the head of Pink Panther's alcohol and other drugs (AOD) team. It looked like Tommy's recent attendance in Buzz Cut, Pink Panther's drug support group, had been a bit patchy.

'Well, if you can attend your next few sessions, we can probably get your AOD counsellor to write a letter of support to show that you're working hard to address your underlying health issues. That way, I might be able to get you a diversion or a good behaviour bond. What do you reckon?'

Tommy nodded. We shook hands, and I hurried back to my desk to officially open my first Queer Legal Service file. *This is great*, I thought. I didn't need to spend hours finding an appropriate health referral to collect evidence to use in court. Health justice partnerships were all the rage in our sector, and I was starting to see why. Pink Panther and I were a one-stop shop.

At eleven a.m., I sat in on a professional development session run by the health promotion team about super gonorrhoea, an antibiotic-resistant strain that was apparently spreading like wildfire in the gay and bi male community. I stared in fear at close-ups of bulbous purple germs with large, waggly spikes, followed by images of red, sore-looking penises and massively swollen testicles. I learnt that super gonorrhoea could also be contracted in the rectum, leading to intense anal itching. I wasn't sure exactly how I would apply this new knowledge in my everyday work, but I felt relieved that I wasn't having sex with any men.

After lunch, I met my second client. Ved was a stunningly handsome young guy from Nepal. He explained to me that he was on a temporary visa while the Department of Home Affairs assessed his claim for asylum on the basis of his sexual orientation. Immigration is one of the few areas of law that you need special qualifications to practise in, and I could have been disbarred if I attempted to help with his protection visa. But from what little I knew of the cruel and harsh Australian immigration system, I didn't like his chances. As I looked into Ved's huge puppy-dog eyes, I felt desperately sad that he'd likely be kicked out eventually.

'Just so you know, I am not qualified to give immigration law advice,' I said.

'It's okay, it's not about that. It's about my job,' Ved said, before explaining that he'd been working cash in hand at a car wash for six weeks. 'But now my boss refuses to pay me, and said I was only on an unpaid trial.'

Employment law was not my forte. I tried to stay away from any area of the law involving money and numbers. Numbers freaked me out. I pulled up the Fair Work Ombudsman website to get some info. After looking through the fact sheet for claiming underpayments, I felt reasonably confident that I could help Ved lodge a claim. But the thought of contacting the government terrified him.

'I don't want to tell them how many hours I worked; it might get me into trouble. I don't want to give them any reason to reject my visa.'

I tried to figure out how many hours he was permitted to work on a temporary protection visa, a task that turned out to be incredibly complicated without seeing his immigration paperwork. The last thing I wanted to do was tell him the wrong thing and get him kicked out of the country.

'Sorry, Ved, but I think you are going to have to talk to an immigration lawyer about this.'

I printed out some fact sheets from Refugee Legal for him and highlighted the two-hour weekly window in which he could try calling their volunteer helpline. As Ved walked out, no closer to getting his money, I felt deflated and out of my depth. I couldn't talk to anyone at Pink Panther about Ved's legal matters due to client confidentiality, so I tried calling Polina. It went to voicemail.

My final appointment of the day was a client called Erica. Her nine-year-old child Fox was assigned male at birth but identified as genderfluid. Erica and the father of her child had separated due to family violence, and Fox was living with Erica. Fox's father believed that Erica was 'brainwashing' Fox into wearing female clothing, so he lodged proceedings in the Family Court to prevent Erica from taking

Fox to a child psychologist with expertise in gender non-conforming children and inclusive care. Erica had engaged a local regional law firm to help her in court, but she felt that her lawyer did not understand Fox's needs and would not be able to put their views to the court appropriately.

By the end of the day, I was exhausted. But I couldn't quite go home yet. I had a meeting booked with Polina and Pink Panther's CEO and his 2IC, neither of whom I'd met before, to finalise the details of the memorandum of understanding between the two organisations.

I hadn't seen a copy of the draft MOU but assumed that this was going to be a friendly meet and greet, given the vibe of the place. But when Neil and his underling Gryn walked into the meeting room where Polina and I were waiting, I realised that I'd been naïve. Neil barely acknowledged my presence, while Gryn subjected me to a bone-crunching handshake from his large, cold hands.

'I've taken the liberty of making a few adjustments,' said Gryn, as he handed Polina a fresh agreement.

She quickly scanned it as I tried to look over her shoulder to follow on.

'That's a bit more than we initially discussed,' Polina said.

'Yes, well, our building costs have gone up a lot recently, so that's the correct cost of the desk rental,' said Gryn.

Desk rental? I thought this was meant to be an extra service for their clients. I'd never heard of a health service charging desk rental to a community legal service before. I didn't want to undermine Polina's position of authority, though, so I kept quiet.

'In any case, Neil and I are double booked, so we'll have to leave you now. Send me an email directly if you have any concerns,' said Gryn, as the two of them got up and left.

Polina and I looked at each other.

'That was a bit weird,' I said.

'Yeah. Are they all like that here?' she asked.

'No, everyone has been really, really nice,' I replied.

'Okay, well, just leave that with me,' Polina said.

I nodded. I was more than happy not to have anything to do with those gays again for as long as I could.

* * *

After work, I entered the waiting room of the Mind Equality Centre in Fitzroy North. This rainbow-branded counselling service was a brand-new offshoot of Mind Australia, one of the largest national mental health organisations. They had received a whole pot of government guilt money post–marriage equality to address the needs of the LGBTIQ community.

I glanced at my phone. *Fuck.* I was already five minutes late. I wasn't quite sure how my transition-related medical appointments were going to fit in around my new full-time job, but I was going to have to make it work.

I walked up to the receptionist, a punky, androgynous person with a lip ring and streaks of blue through their hair.

'I'm Sam. I have a first appointment. Sorry I'm late,' I said.

I felt awkward, unsure if this person in front of me knew that I was here to discuss my gender transition.

They smiled, gave me a clipboard with paperwork to fill in, and directed me to take a seat. The waiting room was appointed with bright, leafy plants in jaunty, colourful self-watering pots. Copies of the gay street press and the queer magazine *Archer* were spread out artfully on the table.

A couple of minutes later, my new gender counsellor Dave strolled out to greet me. He was well over 6 foot, with long limbs and a scraggly red beard. Of all the things I had imagined, a tall dude who looked like strapping, young horticulturalist was not who I had imagined as my guide to being transgender.

'Lovely to meet you, Sam, come in,' Dave said.

Dave. I couldn't believe my gender counsellor was called Dave. I followed Dave into his office. I immediately noted his bookcase, which was full of psychology textbooks and trans memoirs. Nevo Zisin's popular teen memoir *Finding Nevo: How I Confused Everyone* was displayed prominently in the middle of the shelf, red cartoon cover facing outwards.

There was a burnt orange leather couch and two single grey armchairs. I looked up at Dave to see where he'd like me to sit.

'Wherever you feel most comfortable,' he said with a smile.

Was this a test? I wondered. I chose an armchair, and Dave sat on the one opposite.

Once seated, I was able to take in Dave's appearance more clearly. His bright auburn hair was tied back in a tight top bun. His pale skin looked as though it would burn easily.

'So, what can I help you with?' he asked.

I hated this question. Surely he knew exactly what I was here for? He had my new client file right in front of him, which no doubt contained my initial email and intake notes. He just wanted me to come right out and say it.

'I've been told I need to get a letter from a clinical psychologist to get top surgery. So, yeah.'

'Sure. Perhaps we can start by you telling me a little bit about yourself?' Dave said.

God, I really didn't want to get into all this right now. It had been hard enough to work up the nerve to begin transitioning. I didn't seem fair that I be forced to unpack all my childhood gender trauma while working full-time to pay for surgery. Surely there'd be plenty of time for that later?

'Well, I'm thirty-four, I'm a lawyer and I've been on testosterone for a week now,' I replied.

'Wow, that's huge news. Congratulations,' Dave replied.

I was unsure whether he was congratulating me for taking testosterone or for being a lawyer, so I just smiled and waited for him to continue.

'What kind of law do you do?' he asked.

I sighed, uncertain whether I should disclose that I was, in a way, in the same business as him.

'I work at the Queer Legal Service,' I said.

'Wow, that must be challenging. That's two really big things to be doing at once,' he said.

'I guess,' I replied.

We both sat in silence.

'Who prescribed you the hormones?' Dave asked.

I thought back to the slim, silver-haired man in a plum-coloured shirt. His crinkly, smiling eyes and matter-of-fact approach made me feel at ease with my impending life change.

'Dr Levi at the Equinox Trans Health Clinic, just down the road from here, actually' I replied.

'Yes, I know Dr Levi. How did that first appointment make you feel?' Dave asked.

I remembered Dr Levi typing up the prescription. It seemed like no one had ever typed so slowly. I'd had my hands pressed to my knees to stop them from shaking. Sweat had begun to accumulate on my upper lip. When Dr Levi's ageing printer had come to life, whirring and spluttering, and finally spat out the magic document, I felt like I was watching a movie. I couldn't believe that after all these years, I was finally doing it.

'Good, I guess,' I told Dave.

He waited for me to expand on this, but I wasn't taking the bait. I knew I was being emotionally withholding, but I really just wanted to get my surgery letter. It seemed unlikely that Dave had any special insights to assist me with any of this.

Eventually, Dave cracked. 'And how are you feeling about being here today?' he asked.

Embarrassed was the first emotion that came to mind. It was bad enough that I had to talk to anyone about all this, let alone to a tall manly man.

'Um, you know, good?' I replied.

Dave nodded. Then he took out an A4 sheet of paper from a folder on his lap.

'So, perhaps this little fella can help us today,' he said, handing me the piece of paper.

I looked at it. A crudely drawn picture of a prancing unicorn with a rainbow horn grinned back at me. A sash around its cartoon body read, 'The Gender Unicorn'. It stood at the start of a long cobblestone road.

'This is just a tool for us to set out some milestones on your own gender journey so far. Where would you like to start us off?'

I felt mildly patronised by this request. I already felt as though I was far too old to be changing my gender, and the Gender Unicorn was not helping. It was embarrassing to think about going through a second adolescence at my age, when I was closer to menopause than puberty. Not to mention the self-obsessed, narcissistic bubble that I'd noticed most trans people go into in the early stages of their transition.

I dutifully plotted out my personal gender history. Born female in 1983 in a satellite town outside of London. When I was five, I took to telling my playmates that I'd be having a 'sex change' when I turned eighteen. Migrated to Perth, Western Australia, in 1990. Headed east to Melbourne in 2004. Changed my name to Sam in 2008. Started taking testosterone one week ago and counting.

After the success of this first exercise, Dave brought out a second photocopy. I stared down at what I first thought was a cartoon gingerbread man. After re-reading the title, however, I discovered it was not a cartoon gingerbread man at all but 'The Genderbread Person'. The Genderbread Person had a rainbow-coloured brain, which was labelled 'Gender Identity'; a red love heart in the middle of their chest, labelled 'Sexual/Romantic Attraction'; and the combined male, female and androgyne symbols between their legs, labelled 'Anatomical Sex'.

A swirling pattern on the outside of the drawing was labelled 'Gender Expression'.

Beneath was a series of lines linked to the labels. In the first instance, I was to mark my 'Woman-ness' and 'Man-ness' on the Gender Identity spectrum, and then again for 'Feminine' and 'Masculine' under the Gender Expression heading.

I sighed. Decades of impenetrable academic queer theory, starting with Judith Butler's *Gender Trouble*, had slowly filtered down from the academy to this moment, to this inedible piece of genderbread. I obediently marked a series of Xs across the lines to indicate that I identified mainly with 'Man-ness', that I presented in a masculine way and that my anatomical sex was squarely female. I put an X in the middle section of sexual attraction and towards the female end of romantic attachment.

I looked up at Dave, who was peering down at my genderbread person.

'Wow, you finished that off quickly. Did it bring anything up for you?' he asked.

I didn't want to offend him by saying that I thought this whole process was an infantilising load of shit, so I tried to think of something more constructive.

'It kinda reminds me of the Raggy Dolls,' I said.

'What's that?' Dave asked.

I stared at Dave. Of course he didn't know about the Raggy Dolls. When did everyone suddenly start being younger than me? Why couldn't I have had a nice trans woman in her sixties or something, instead of this big goof?

'It was just a British kids' TV show from the '80s. They were toys that had been thrown into a reject bin, who then come to life and have adventures. One of them had their head on backwards, and there was Sad Sack, who was kind of just a fat little teddy bear in a bow tie with depression. Like Eeyore, I guess.'

'And did you identify with them because you felt different?' Dave asked.

My mind snapped to my recurring childhood nightmares, which I had every few months for four years, beginning when I was five years old. I would be standing at the top of a staircase, peering down. On the left was a crowd of males, yelling, banging drums and tearing up thick brown boxes. On the right-hand side stood the females, holding earrings and necklaces and clanging musical triangles. In my dream, I didn't go anywhere or do anything. I was just stuck on that precipice, facing two sets of different but equally unbearable sounds and textures. The feeling cleaved my mind in half, and I would wake up in tears.

'Yeah, I guess so,' I said.

I suddenly felt a hot rush of annoyance at having to go through all this with Dave. I was only here because Dr Levi had told me it was a condition of my top surgery that I get a letter confirming that I meet the clinical criteria for gender dysphoria. I needed a letter from one man to tell another man that he was free to charge me $10,000 to remove my breasts. It all felt galling.

'And what kind of toys did you play with?' Dave asked.

I knew we'd end up here.

I had a sip of water, then took Dave through the list of toys I'd played with as a kid. Little green soldiers, plastic dinosaurs, Lego, Transformers. Professional wrestling figurines. I was basically a walking transmasculine cliché.

Finally, our first session came to an end. Just four more sessions to go before I could get my top surgery letter. I picked up my heavy backpack, stuffed with my chunky Dell and fresh client files. I exited back out onto St Georges Road. The sun was starting to set, but it was still light. I loved being back out on the street, just another anonymous member of Melbourne's inner-north crowd. I felt like I could breathe again.

* * *

I caught the train home from Rushall to Spotswood Station. As soon as my feet hit the platform, the wafting smell of rotten eggs mixed with kerosene filled my nostrils. There must've been another spill in one of the huge tanks at Mobil's Altona refinery. I'd just moved to the west from Coburg, into a share house with a lesbian couple, Enid and Sissie, and their two dogs, Bobo and Moxie. Bobo was a huge, grey, lumbering Irish wolfhound while Moxie was a tiny, hairless Chinese Crested dog. I found Moxie's mottled pink-and-black nude flesh almost as disturbing as his prominent mushroom-coloured penile sheath, which was comically large in comparison to the rest of his body.

The house was a fixer-upper that Sissie's parents had just bought for her to live in. Despite their relative wealth, the housing market was so hot that they could only afford a place in the undesirable end of Yarraville, next to the freeway, amongst vestiges of the last remining industrial workshops in the inner west. The windows were unsealed and there were cracks in the corner of my bedroom, stuffed with alfoil to try to keep the elements out. But my standards were not high. I just wanted to live anywhere close to Gemma that would let me keep Tibby, my ageing fluffy black mutt. Gemma and I had met a few months ago at a Legal Aid function when I'd sat down next to her by chance. I'd been instantly charmed by her tirade against public funding for private schools and tales of her volunteer work at an anti–death penalty clinic in New Orleans. Unlike me, who had stumbled somewhat unwillingly into the law, Gemma was a born advocate, with unending passion for debate and social justice. I never had to worry about what to say when I was out with Gemma, because no one was paying any attention to me. She was charming, gregarious and a natural entertainer. With her around, I could relax and fade into the background.

When I'd moved in, the agreement was that I'd have the front two rooms and my own bathroom, almost like a granny flat. Unfortunately, Bobo liked nothing more than sleeping on the couch in 'my end' of the house. As soon as I'd leave for the day, he'd inevitably push the flimsy dividing door open and go to sleep in his preferred spot in the morning sun. This in itself didn't bother me, except for the fact that it gave Moxie ample opportunity to undertake his preferred activity, which was to shit on my bath mat. Over and over again I'd get home, rush to use the toilet, only to find myself standing on tiny, squished Chinese Crested dog poo. It made me enraged out of all proportion. I began to wonder if my fury was an effect of the testosterone. Tibby didn't like living with Bobo and Moxie either. I realised it had been a mistake as soon as I'd moved in, but I didn't want to offend Sissie and Enid by moving out immediately. I figured I'd have to stay a minimum of six months so as not to cause offence.

I trekked down past the coffee shops and bourgie bakeries on Hudson's Road and under the Westgate Bridge, the roaring sound of cars thundering overhead. Between the refinery, the all-night truck fumes and a recent industrial accident that had poisoned all the fish in the local creek, I did wonder how many months I was shaving off my lifespan by living out here.

I took Tibby for a walk along a wild part of Cruikshank Park at the end of our dead-end street. There, a storm drain filled with chaotic neon graffiti called my name. I climbed down to get a better look. Tibby raced through the 50-metre-long drain, her paws flicking up mud as she went, as I took in the kaleidoscope of multi-coloured obscenities. When I returned, Gemma pulled up in her silver Mazda with a box of fresh fruit and vegies from her family's shop. We kissed and swapped tales from our respective work days, before heading into the kitchen to make dinner. As I reached into the top cupboard to find pasta, an unfamiliar smell tickled Gemma's nose.

'What's that? Are you wearing Lynx?' she asked.

'It's not Lynx, it's Men's Dove,' I said, scowling defensively.

'God, that's triggering. It smells like a boy's locker room.'

For some time, I'd been fixated on wearing the few unisex-branded deodorants available that were exclusively natural, chemical-free options. Since I'd started taking testosterone, I'd starting sweating more than ever. The crystals were simply not up to the task of neutralising my increasingly offensive body odour. I'd carefully looked over all the options at Footscray Coles to find the one with the least obnoxious, hyper-masculine marketing. I thought it smelt okay.

'Do you really have to start wearing men's deodorant? What happened to smashing gender stereotypes?' Gemma asked.

I felt a surge of adrenaline.

'Why's it my job to smash them? Why don't you tell your dad or your brother to stop wearing men's deodorant and then maybe I will,' I replied.

I chucked the bag of pasta onto the counter and stalked off to the bathroom. I couldn't remember when I'd last been so angry. Gemma knocked on the door, full of apologies, but I didn't let her in. Instead, I unlocked the bathroom door, took Tibby back down to the creek and listened to another true crime podcast in the dark, leaving Gemma to cook dinner alone.

Chapter 3
(You're the) Trans Voice

I was back at La Trobe Uni in Bundoora, almost a decade to the day since I'd watched my last essay flutter into the submissions chute in the Law building. I'd never had a reason to enter the Health Sciences building before, though. When I finally identified it from amongst the many other grey brutalist buildings, I made my way up to level four. There, I found the plain Jane waiting room of the transgender speech pathology clinic.

Despite my increasingly surly, petulant behaviour, Gemma insisted on driving me the 30 kilometres north of the city before she started work because she knew how anxious driving made me. I felt awkward and guilty about my increasing emotional reliance on Gemma. We hadn't been together for very long when I announced I was going to transition. The two of us had been on a romantic getaway in Sydney. On a whim we'd gone to see a feminist comedy at Carriageworks called *Wild Bore*. I'd laughed along as the three female performers had roasted their critics, right until an unexpected fourth actor appeared for the final act. It was Krishna Istha, a young trans masculine comedian. They were dressed in a pleated black skirt, sneakers and a colourful, over-sized t-shirt that looked like it was from the boys' section of Kmart. They returned fire at the comedians, pointing out their smug cultural assumptions and blind spots. But I could barely follow. Instead, I was reeling from the shock of seeing a trans masculine person on stage for the first time in my life, especially since I had not been forewarned. I did my best to breathe steadily and maintain a mask of detached amusement. But I was sent into a fresh wave of panic when all four performers started dancing completely naked, barring Krishna's tan-coloured binder. As I watched their nude, slim, masculine form, with a simple dark pubic mound where one might've expected a penis and testicles to be, I suppressed an urge to bolt from the theatre altogether. How could they be so carefree?

That night, I woke up next to Gemma in our unfamiliar Airbnb, bawling my eyes out. Krishna's performance had shaken something loose inside me. What amount of bravery had it taken them to appear naked onstage like that, and why didn't I possess an ounce of their courage? It suddenly seemed obvious to me that I could live my life the way I wanted to – the only thing holding me back was myself.

I shook Gemma awake and told her my decision. After this dramatic disclosure, I felt strangely calm, like a weight had been lifted from my shoulders. But my news seemed to elicit the very opposite reaction in Gemma. She began to cry. She was still getting used to being in her first same-sex romance, and now had to grapple with a whole new set of issues. It was a lot of pressure to put on a brand-new relationship.

I sat in the speech pathology waiting room, thinking about just how supportive and open-minded Gemma had become. I got out the notes app on my phone and wrote a reminder to be less of a dickhead to her.

A few minutes later, a woman in her early thirties with long, curly brown hair wearing a delightfully soft-looking orange-and-pink scarf came to collect me.

'Sam? I'm Emily,' she said.

I smiled and followed her into a small, windowless medical office with a sink and an examination table. She showed me an anatomical picture of a larynx. Between the epiglottis, vocal cords, trachea and cartilage, it looked like a cross between a printed lipstick kiss and a vagina.

'I am sure you've done your own research, Sam, but I'd like to start by covering the basics,' Emily said.

I smiled and nodded.

'So, the first thing to note is that the larynx is generally smaller in females than in males. A compact larynx means females also have a shorter vocal tract and slight vocal folds. They also have less thyroid cartilage protecting the larynx, all of which give them a higher-pitched voice.'

She then pointed to the vocal cords.

'Female vocal folds are thinner and shorter, so they create a higher sound when air flows by. The triangular cross-section shape of the vocal folds allows for more vibration, elevating the pitch. This is in contrast to males, who have thicker, longer vocal folds that produce a lower tone.'

I nodded, eager to appear as though I understood.

'Testosterone tends to make most people's vocal cords thicker, producing a lower pitch. So, most trans men find that the testosterone does a lot of the work for them. But it doesn't work for everyone, so we can help you train your own voice to be deeper, if that's the outcome you are looking for,' Emily said.

'Why doesn't it work for some people?' I asked.

'Some find that their bodies are physiologically insensitive to testosterone,' Emily said.

She then asked me how long I'd been taking testosterone. When I told her it had been about a month, she looked at me sympathetically.

'Well, your voice will probably go down yet.'

I hadn't even considered that it might not. I'd mainly been concerned about ending up with what I secretly called 'trans voice', the androgynous, thin, muffled voices that I sometimes found hard to hear. Now it seemed that even getting 'trans voice' would be a massive win. How depressing.

'Now, let's assess where you are at today, so we can track your progress,' said Emily, handing me a photocopy of a page from a science textbook to read into a microphone.

I quickly scanned the page before beginning to read aloud. '"The scaly-breasted lorikeet is an Australian lorikeet found in woodland in eastern Australia. The common name aptly describes this bird, which has yellow breast feathers broadly edged with green that look like scales" ... Should I continue?' I asked.

Emily nodded.

'Scaly-breasted lorikeets are extremely noisy birds and attract attention by their screeching and chattering. The contact call of these birds is a metallic, rolling, continuous screech in flight. They have a shrill chatter when feeding. While resting, they have a soft, gentle twitter. Although, these birds can be quite noisy as mating season draws nearer. These birds are often making loud tweets/squawks when looking for their food,' I read.

'Okay great, that's enough,' said Emily. 'Now tell me how you travelled to this appointment today.'

'I caught the train into town from Footscray, and then got the 250.'

This was a bald-faced lie. I'd spent so much of my life editing out my same-sex partners in polite conversation that I often did it before I'd had a chance to think it through. *This is another way that you are a cunt to Gemma*, I thought to myself.

'And what did you have for breakfast?' Emily asked.

'Vegemite toast and coffee.'

True.

'Okay, give me five while I crunch the numbers.'

As she tapped away on her computer, I turned to look at my surrounds. I noticed for the first time that there was a one-way mirror in the corner of the room. I'd signed a consent form to say that Health Sciences students could observe any of my appointments. I'd thought it was the right thing to do, for the betterment of the next generation of trans healthcare providers, but now I was having doubts. Were they laughing at me over there, nudging each other about yet another lesbian who wanted to be a man?

'So, adult females generally have an average pitch of 175 to 250 hertz, while male adults average 80 to 150 hertz. Your voice is currently at 220.'

Fuck, I thought. Despite rubbing testosterone into my skin every day, my voice was still squarely in the female range. Was I applying it wrong?

'It was a bit deeper when you were reading off the page,' Emily continued, 'and higher when you were telling me about your morning. That shows that if you are more mindful about how you are projecting your voice, you could get it a bit lower.'

With that, we moved on to the first of a series of exercises. Emily directed me to put a straw in my mouth and slowly exhale while making an 'eeee' sound.

I felt ridiculous. I was highly attuned to my unseen, youthful audience behind the one-way mirror. I felt like an exhibit in a nineteenth-century freak show. Emily told me to hum low notes, and then to sing 'ah' and 'oh' as deeply as I could. We ended on a low growling noise. I sounded like a cat in heat.

As she wound up our introductory session, Emily sent me a link to a voice pitch analyser that I could download onto my phone to track my progression. The assigned text to track the pitch of my voice was *The Picture of Dorian Gray*, which I hadn't read since I was in high school. Would my transformation be as dramatic as Dorian's moral decay?

I exited the Health Sciences building and breathed in the crisp autumn air, before heading off to find a coffee, anxious to slip back into being an anonymous member of the public after such scrutiny. I walked into what had once been the student food cooperative. Now a chain burger bar, I was sceptical about the quality of their coffee, but it was long after lunchtime and nowhere else was open. The young woman at the counter was decked out in an embroidered, floral boho dress, and had presumably chosen to play the Leonard Cohen album coming from a Sonos wall speaker. As I ordered a coffee, hyper-conscious of my squeaky Mickey Mouse voice, Leonard Cohen sang in a rasping baritone in the background. It felt like a sign.

When we'd first arrived in Western Australia from England, my family had spent seemingly endless hours in the hot Perth sun, driving around looking for a plot of land to build a house on in the newly cleared outer suburbs. My mum would put on one of her few cassette tapes, inevitably either Leonard Cohen or Elvis Costello, and I'd sit in the back of our second-hand Hyundai, imagining that it was me on stage singing in a low timbre to an audience sipping cocktails in a smoky bar somewhere.

I received my burnt coffee with a smile then walked to the bus stop, only to find that the buses had been cancelled due to industrial action. *Good for them*, I thought. I knocked back my foul brew and trudged up the hill to the tram stop on Plenty Road. I'd only ever caught this slow, meandering tram to and from uni when I was so broke that I couldn't afford a bus ticket. I'd watch the tram doors like a hawk for ticket inspectors in their floor-length black coats. Later, when they started employing plain-clothed inspectors, I'd get off the tram whenever I saw anyone over the age of sixteen get on wearing a baseball cap. This had only made the journey even longer, and I'd started missing more classes than usual. I hadn't been much of a Law student. I'd yawned equally through the Law of Contracts as I had through the definitions of *mens rea* and *beyond reasonable doubt* in Criminal Law. Not that any of my lecturers would have recognised me; I was hardly a diligent student. I'd spent my nights smoking out the front of every queer night north of Gertrude Street and smuggling in concealed silver bladders of Fruity Lexia. Three weeks before the end of every semester, I'd freak out and curse myself for not dropping out before the census date. After a week of angst, I'd finally submit to the process, turning up to the Borchardt Library and borrowing an out-of-date textbook before locking myself in my bedroom for two weeks to cram for exams in subjects I barely knew I'd been enrolled in. My knowledge of everything from Constitutional Law to the Law of Torts was surface at best, but it was enough for me to attain a bog standard 65 per cent course average. I soon realised that the whole concept of the law of precedent meant that conservatism and looking reverently at the past was effectively baked into the system.

If I'd learnt anything about LGBTIQ law during my time at La Trobe, I didn't remember it. The few pieces of case law that still swirled around in my head from uni were the wacky historical ones, like *Donoghue v Stevenson*. Mrs Donoghue sued a ginger beer manufacturer after she found a decomposing snail inside her drink. I also remembered *Carlill v the Carbolic Smoke Ball Company*, a case about a hyped-up advertisement for a dodgy flu remedy, because it hinged on the definition of the term 'mere puffery'. I thought that 'Mia Puffery' would make a great stage name for a drag queen at our end-of-year Law Ball, an event which I never attended, of course.

As the end of my degree grew nearer, I still had no idea what I would do afterwards. I hadn't done any summer clerkships and couldn't imagine myself ever working for a big law firm. I was never going to be able to look the part. Women were expected to have impeccable hair and wear expensive pantsuits. I didn't even own a suit, and certainly couldn't afford one from anywhere other than an op shop. It seemed like you could probably be a lesbian in a law firm, but you'd have to be a very well-dressed one. I was poor and sloppy. Strange to think that over a decade later, I was now Melbourne's very own specialist LGBTIQ lawyer.

After sliding into a seat on the tram, I tapped out a few emails on my personal phone, which I then emailed to myself to forward to clients from my ancient work flip phone. Engrossed in this task, it was only when we passed the Wesley Anne, a high-roofed timber and stone bar in Northcote, that I looked up.

On the evening after my final exam, my friends and I had gone to the Wesley Anne to celebrate. We'd laughed and made stupid law jokes, and I'd felt both sad and glad that this was the end. We'd kept drinking in the alleyway outside my friend's flat. A bottle of vodka was procured. We drank a lot of it and at some point, to prove my strength, I'd challenged my friend Kyle to a fight. Kyle, who had 9 inches and at least 20 kilos on me, laughed it off at first. But I'd insisted. I offered to punch him once and then he could punch me back. We'd taken turns hitting each other until one of us gave up.

I was so drunk I couldn't really feel how hard Kyle's blows were. I punched him as hard as I could, and he just chuckled. Barely a scratch. We kept going until someone insisted that I sit down. When I woke up the next day, I was black and blue. Huge bruises all over my body. It hurt to walk. Fortunately, there weren't any on my face or arms, just my chest and my shoulders. I could barely lift my arms. I didn't want to leave my bedroom because I didn't want to show anyone how much I'd willingly got myself bashed up. I lay in bed on my own, gulping down water and Nurofen, only scuttling out to go to the toilet when my flatmates left the house.

As the tram rattled down High Street into Westgarth, where I finally glimpsed the city, I wondered how many other stupid things I'd done over the years in misguided attempts to embody masculinity?

Tram inspectors got on at the bottom of Smith Street. They had a whole new black paramilitary attire on. I felt an initial flush of anxiety before reminding myself that I was no longer a broke student, but a qualified lawyer with a full-time job and a valid tram ticket. After I showed the inspectors my Myki, though, I surreptitiously took a pic and posted it on a Facebook page that let people know where the tram police were.

When we reached town, I got off the tram on the corner of Bourke and Swanston streets and made my way to Joy 94.9, Melbourne's queer radio station. The station was in a high-rise Melbourne City Council building. I pressed the ground-floor buzzer to get let into the building, while staring, briefly mesmerised, at the kangaroo and koala tourist souvenirs out the front of the adjacent duty-free gift shop, specialising in ugg boots, opals and powdered milk.

After a couple of minutes, someone finally answered the call bell and granted me access to the lift. I hit the button for level nine and popped out in the Joy lobby moments later. No one was around, so I sat on a couch and flicked through the gay street press. In between scene photographs of topless twinks at Poof Doof, there was a brief explainer on the Religious Discrimination Bill, which Prime Minister Malcolm Turnbull had just introduced. It was widely considered to be a concession to the Christian Right, who were still dirty about losing the marriage equality plebiscite.

I placed some flyers that I'd made about the Queer Legal Service on the waiting room table, amidst other colourful flyers for health services and coming out support groups. A couple of minutes later, one of the presenters gestured for me to come into the studio. She had long blonde hair and the polished look of a Human Resources consultant – not at all the kind of woman I expected to see at a queer community radio station..

She invited me to sit in front of a fluffy black microphone and put on headphones. A younger man with gelled-up blonde hair was pressing buttons on the station panel, while an older man with a short white beard and a heavy gold ring looked up from his newspaper and nodded at me.

'On in fifteen seconds,' the younger man brusquely told us, while play-ing an advert for a cosmetic clinic in Prahran.

To the listeners, he purred, 'You're on Joy 94.9, Australia's only dedi-cated rainbow radio station, bringing you fresh and uplifting beats all day and all night.'

'Now joining us in the studio,' said the older man, 'is Sam Elkin, a lawyer at the brand-new Queer Legal Service. Sam, I hear you are a transgender lawyer. What's that like?'

'Great!' I managed to splutter out, before pivoting the conversation to anything other than myself. *What a stupid fucking question*, I thought.

'So, do you do gay divorces?' asked the guy with frosted tips. 'That'll be the next big thing now that marriage equality has passed!'

The three of them burst into laughter. I smiled and tried my best to titter along with them.

'Yes, we are certainly pleased that same-sex marriage has passed, but no, divorces aren't something we do. But we can help with family violence and intervention orders,' I replied.

The three of them looked at me, stumped for quips.

'We help LGBTIQ Victorians who are financially disadvantaged with a range of criminal, civil and family law issues,' I said, glad to have got my key line out.

'Sam, what about this transgender woman's football case? What are your thoughts on the AFL's decision to rule Hannah Mouncey ineligi-ble for the AFLW draft?' the bald man asked.

I hadn't prepared for this total change in direction. The AFL had just refused to allow trans athlete Hannah Mouncey from nominating for the pre-season AFLW draft. In doing so, they'd relied on an exemption in the *Equal Opportunity Act* that allowed them to discriminate where 'strength, stamina or physique is relevant'. I felt torn between speaking as a lawyer and speaking on my own behalf. Whose opinion were they asking?

'I think that it's very sad that the AFL came out in support of marriage equality last year, but are now denying one single trans athlete her dream of playing in the new national competition,' I said.

The hosts nodded sympathetically before dropping a fresh commercial dance track. As quickly as it had begun, my public grilling was now over. I went back down in the lift and was soon spat out into the street.

As I made my way down Bourke Street, I thought to myself, *That didn't feel good.* I was only meant to be going on to spruik the legal service. I felt strangely used and exploited, like a gunky tissue.

But there was no time to dwell on it. My next stop was a University Law building on Lonsdale Street, where I'd been invited by the Queer Law Students' Association to sit on a panel about LGBTIQ inclusion in the law. I felt exhausted and admonished myself for ever having agreed to it when I had actual client work to do. I'd been asked by a third-year Law student who identified as non-binary. When the student told me how much it would mean to them to have a real-life trans lawyer speak to their group, I felt like I couldn't say no.

By the time I got there, I was sweaty, thirsty and needed to go to the toilet. But there was no time to address any of that. The emcee stuck a name tag and pronoun badge on me and whisked me up on stage. There, I appeared beside a gay man in his fifties who was a partner in a commercial law firm and a young, short-haired female police officer from Frankston Station, who was representing the LGBTIQ liaison officer program. I couldn't think of anything that bound the three of us together ideologically, and I felt particularly annoyed that Beanie hadn't told me I'd be sharing the stage with a cop, no matter how well-intentioned she might be. In my last job, as a criminal duty lawyer at Legal Aid, it was necessary to have almost daily contact with police prosecutors. I'd send long emails day after day, pleading for the cops to withdraw charges or offer teenage offenders a diversion. The response was always the same: 'Request denied.' I had been looking forward to not having to interact with them for a while.

The commercial law partner explained to the students that it was fine to be gay at his work now, and that they should all consider coming and doing a summer clerkship with his firm. The police officer discussed careers in the police force and explained the LGBTIQ liaison officer program. I'd never found the liaison officers at all helpful. Whenever I'd tried to refer a client to them, their phone was inevitably switched off or they were out on patrol. As far as I could tell, their main job was to apologise for the behaviour of their piggish colleagues and be wheeled out to provide positive comms during Midsumma. But it didn't seem like the right time for me to mention any of that.

When it was my turn to spruik my part of the legal profession, I looked into the eager eyes of the law students.

'Community legal centres were set up in the 1970s to provide free legal assistance to people who couldn't afford it. In any given week I'll help public housing tenants, new migrants and sex workers. We agitate for changes to unjust laws and run free community legal education sessions about renters' rights and how to self-represent in court. It's not glamorous, but you get to work with people and feel a sense of achievement.'

Some students looked interested in volunteering, so I handed around a few flyers.

When the panel finished up, it was almost two o'clock. I was busting to go to the toilet but felt weird about using the bathrooms at the law school, in case I bumped into one of the students. Instead, I headed to the public toilets on Collins Street below the Melbourne Town Hall. On a whim, I decided that today would be the day that I would use the men's room. I'd been wanting to since I started taking testosterone but kept chickening out at the last minute. Not today. If I could talk to students and any random tuned in to Joy 94.9 about being trans-gender, surely I could take this next step? I felt terrified as I entered this forbidden, gender-segregated space. Then the odour of shit, stale piss and urinal cakes hit me. I sat down in a stall then relieved myself, while reading a government poster about the importance of prostate cancer screenings. *This is my prize*, I thought. As I was washing my hands, an elderly man walked in. He took no notice of me at all as he unzipped and began using the urinal. I held my head up high when I ascended out of the men's toilets and back onto the street. I was a gender bender, like Virginia Woolf's Orlando. Or a clownfish.

While sitting on the near-empty tram on the way to Pink Panther, I opened the voice app and quietly read aloud an excerpt from *The Picture of Dorian Gray*. As I struggled over Wilde's verbose prose describing the delicate beauty of honey-coloured flowers in full blossom, as observed by the camp, chain-smoking Lord Henry Wotton, I was stung by the written confirmation of what I already knew: still female.

Chapter 4
Let Her Play

Hannah Mouncey was still all over the news, and everyone had an opinion. Some saw the AFL's decision to refuse to allow her to play as an infuriating about-face for a league that had just campaigned for marriage equality. Others pointed to Mouncey's 190-centimetre height and 100-kilo weight as conclusive evidence that she should never be allowed to play in the women's league. Right-wing commentators saw the push for her to join the AFLW as confirmation of the 'slippery slope' effect of same-sex marriage, and evidence of the 'transgender agenda' to impose radical gender ideology on mainstream Australia.

As I was reading some particularly vile comments underneath one such article, I received an unexpected phone call. Would I like to participate in an AFL consultation about its policy on transgender participation? Startled and a little suspicious, I asked them to send me the details while I mulled over the invitation.

In the early 1990s, I'd copied my brother by becoming a fan of the West Coast Eagles after we migrated to Perth. They were the newest team in the comp, and on the ascent. Everyone in WA except for my parents, who loathed all sport, seemed to have got behind them. Yellow and blue flags hung on every house during their finals runs in those years. My brother treasured his Peter Sumich, Chris Mainwaring and Guy McKenna footy cards. Watching AFL games on Channel 7 on the weekend was a huge part of our cultural assimilation. But when I hit my teens, rape allegations against several West Coast players turned me right off them, and the sport in general.

I looked at the consultation invite, which had been promptly emailed to me. It was to be held at Marvel Stadium, which I'd been to many times with Gemma and her family over the last few months to watch the Western Bulldogs play, the team they were fanatical about. I had been enjoying getting back on the AFL bandwagon. I loved watching the players perform bone-crunching tackles before leaping right up to spin, run and jump for the ball. It was an incredible spectacle of relentless human effort. I hated it when players got injured and were eventually replaced by younger, fresh-faced ones, an endless conveyer belt that even the gifted athletes eventually fell off the end of. I enjoyed the ritual of dressing up in team colours and perusing endless varieties of beanies and scarves at the merch stand at half-time. But more than anything, I liked that it didn't really matter. In the endless news cycle of war, catastrophic climate change and the horrors of Australia's offshore detention regime, reading the sports pages was a blessed treat.

But I was still suspicious of the AFL as an institution. Indigenous footballer Adam Goodes had been hounded out of the game by racism, and former footballers were always turning up in the media to say something deeply racist or sexist. The idea that they'd do a better job with trans issues seemed remote.

But it was at Marvel Stadium. And I was flattered that anyone in the AFL cared about my opinion.

The next Monday I woke up, had a shower, and then got out my beloved testosterone cream. The container looked like a toothpaste tube, so I was careful to store it under the sink to take away the risk of Gemma or me accidentally brushing our teeth with it. The two main ways of taking testosterone were via quarterly injections or by daily application of a cream. I figured that it was better to start with the cream, so I could stop immediately if I changed my mind at any point. I still wasn't sure if I wanted to 'go the whole hog' with my transition or whether a more androgynous appearance and voice would help me feel more comfortable. That's why I'd started on a quarter dose.

The medication wasn't designed for people like me, but for men whose testicles were not producing enough testosterone. The instructions recommended applying the cream to my balls. As this was obviously not on the cards, I carefully drew out 0.5 millilitres with a measuring applicator and rubbed it onto my torso. There, the testosterone would seep through my skin and into my bloodstream. Applying the opaque, odourless balm was painless. I nonetheless treated it like a hazardous material, as I'd been sternly warned by Dr Levi about the risks of unintentional testosterone transfer onto Gemma.

We caught the train into the city together, forcing ourselves into a packed carriage at Middle Footscray. I got off at Southern Cross and headed by foot into Docklands. The windy city enclave, full of towering, half-empty glass apartments, would've looked more at home on the Gold Coast than in Melbourne. I arrived at Marvel and stood by the tiny door on the edge of the gargantuan stadium, following the directions on the invite. I was early, and at that moment it seemed incredulous to me that anyone would ever come and get me. Perhaps it had all been a joke? But then a trans woman in her fifties, wearing a purple overcoat and a rainbow scarf, came around the corner, smoking a cigarette. I introduced myself. Deirdre explained that she'd just arrived on an early morning flight from Launceston. The next person to arrive was Griffin, a short, muscular young trans guy who played for the Darebin Falcons in the local women's footy comp. Griffin was soon joined by his partner, a non-binary player in the same comp. I turned back to Deirdre and asked her if she played football too, in an effort to make conversation.

'Are you kidding? I'd rather die,' she said, stubbing out her cigarette. 'I just said yes to get a free flight over to Melbourne. I've been invited to pitch my screenplay to a production company but haven't had the cash to get here.'

'What's your movie about?' I asked.

'An intergalactic soap opera set on Venus and Mars. With an all-trans cast, of course,' Deirdre said.

I grinned. I wanted to see that movie.

As the minutes ticked by, more and more trans people turned up, shivering in the unseasonably cold weather. Finally, the big metal door swung open, and a woman in a lush grey suit appeared before us.

'Great to see you all. I'm Mandy, the consultant who'll be working with you today. Come on in,' she said.

We all shuffled in behind Mandy and followed her through a series of identical grey corridors. I was highly attuned to the fact that I was shoulder to shoulder with more trans people than I ever had been before. It felt like my first day of high school. We continued to weave through walkways before eventually popping out into a huge conference room with blue-and-green swirling carpet. It looked like somewhere between an open-plan office and a daggy wedding reception centre.

Huge floor-to-ceiling windows revealed the warm green of the pristine footy field. Even though we were here to talk about something very serious, I was momentarily overtaken by wonder at the spectacular view.

'Right this way,' Mandy said, beckoning us into a meeting room.

Inside were tables with crisp white tablecloths, with official AFL pens and notepads at every seat. The indoor pot plants were so green they were probably fake. I sat down at a table near the back of the room, in front of the impressive spread of morning tea, and watched the tables slowly fill up. Even though I'd already had breakfast, I was starving, another effect of the testosterone. I grabbed a freshly baked blueberry muffin and ate it as quickly as I could, hoping that no one else would notice. Unfortunately, I got crumbs all over the table. I looked down at the carpet. The design was either an abstract rendering of grapes and blades of grass or stylised vomit. Either way, it was perfect for hiding my mess, which I quietly wiped onto the floor. As AFL representatives wearing colourful lanyards milled around at the back of the room, Mandy and another corporate-looking type with an artfully cut bob strode to the front to set up their PowerPoint presentation. The woman with the bob looked up from her computer and gave me a big grin.

'Sam? How are you? I'm Mem, I went to uni with Gemma. I see you on her Instagram all the time,' she said.

I smiled and walked over to say hello. She told me she was working for one of the big Melbourne law firms, and that they'd been contracted by the AFL to develop their inaugural gender diversity policy.

'It's such an honour to work with you on something big and important like this,' Mem said.

I nodded, uncertain if she knew how much resentment there was in the room towards this process. She continued to make polite small talk with me. This was not a good start. I was already looking like a turncoat, fraternising with the enemy. Just as I was making a move to sit back down, Hannah Mouncey walked in.

So much had been written about her in the newspapers that she seemed like a celebrity to me. She was a celebrity, I supposed, just without any of the usual attendant financial benefits. She was tall with neat, straightened blonde hair, wearing a chic, modest black dress. All eyes were immediately upon her. People came over to offer her hugs and words of support. I thought about going over, but I felt too awkward. I didn't want her to feel mobbed. Besides, who was I? She didn't even know me.

Mem and Mandy began the presentation, a slick, uninformative slide show about the AFL's commitment to equality and its vision for a future of community inclusion.

We then worked on a 'group agreement' for forty-five minutes, where we agreed that we'd all be respectful and tolerant of each other's views. We had a break for morning tea, and then a session where we had to come up with a shared vision statement outlining what we wanted from an inclusive AFL. I wondered when we were going to get onto the actual issue at hand, which was the rules around whether trans women would be allowed to play in the AFLW.

As Mandy wrapped up the presentation, Mem began handing out copies of a draft thirty-page policy that an underling had just rushed in on photocopy paper that was still warm. Had someone still been writing it until moments ago, with all the palaver about a group agreement just to stall for time?

'This is the draft policy that we want to work through with you today,' said Mem, 'just as a starting point. I'm going to collect them at the end of the session.'

'Now, we'll give you five minutes and then we will come back to discuss,' Mandy said.

I put my hand up.

'It's difficult to give meaningful feedback on a document you've only had time to skim over. Could we have a bit longer to read it?' I asked.

The two conferred with the lurking AFL representatives. They agreed we could have a bit longer with the document if we were willing to give up one of our afternoon tea breaks.

'Before we take this time,' said Mem, 'it's important that I emphasis to you that the AFL wants this to be a good faith process. If anyone leaks this draft, work-in-progress document to the media, it will inevitably damage the trans and gender-diverse community's relationship with the AFL. And no one wants that, obviously.'

All eyes were again on Hannah.

And then we were given time to peruse the draft policy. I felt like this was my moment to be useful, that it was my responsibility with my training to try to absorb this entire document in the short amount of time allocated to us, so that we could ask meaningful questions. It felt like uni exam conditions. I was desperate to do my bit.

I wrote down information about the maximum testosterone levels that a female or non-binary player was allowed to have, and the proposed testing to ensure that they would not have a competitive advantage. I noted that it explicitly stated that trans women were allowed to play AFL at the community level, as players could not be excluded for having a competitive advantage there. This seemed counterintuitive to me – surely players at the lower levels were more likely to be injured by those with a so-called 'competitive advantage' than an elite player, who would be faster, stronger and trained to avoid injury?

'Okay, everyone, time's up,' Mem said, as she came back around and swept up our papers. 'We'll now break out into small groups and write our ideas and comments on butcher's paper. Please choose one person from your group to present back to the room,' Mem said.

I gravitated towards Deirdre, as I was eager to hear what she thought about it all. We went around in a group to share our thoughts, while I wrote their words on the butcher's paper.

'I don't know why anyone would want to play a game like this, where your head is likely to get pummelled into the ground,' Deirdre said, 'but these policies seem more like exclusion than inclusion to me.'

She sure had a way with words.

A tall, non-binary person called Pyke spoke next. They had long, dyed-red hair and wore thick black glasses.

'All this will do is drive trans women away from the game. All that testing? It's so unfair. We've already got high suicide rates and poor health, why do they want to make it even harder for us?' Pyke said.

Everyone in the group nodded, as I wrote down what Pyke said as quickly as I could.

'It seems like this gives this shadowy sub-committee, who ultimately get to decide, way too much discretion. How would we ever know if the trans player has met the requirements or not?' someone else said.

'Okay, folks, I can hear some very productive discussions happening at the table. We're going to wind up now, so please bring your pieces of paper to the front of the room,' said Mem.

As I dropped off our pieces of butcher's paper, I glanced at what the other groups had written down.

I've received death threats and threats from people saying they are going to get my kids taken off me, all for playing footy as a trans woman. What is the AFL doing about that?

This will make trans kids feel unwelcome at the footy.

'Will we be talking through our comments?' someone asked.

'No time, I'm afraid,' Mem said.

'We'll get them typed up ASAP, though,' Mandy added, 'and they'll be incorporated into our thinking into the second draft.'

'We thank you for being so generous in sharing your experience, expertise and perspectives,' Mem said.

I left that day feeling sad, confused and vaguely complicit in a process that wasn't going to assist Hannah or any other trans women who wanted to play in the AFLW in future. On the way out, I walked past the Marvel Stadium posters for *Thor*. Hannah was a bit like a super-hero: big and strong, brave and articulate, ready to stand up in the face of all that was wrong in the world to pursue her dream. There were villains galore, from Sam Newman to the shadowy decision-makers who made the call to deny her entry into the first AFLW draft. If this was a superhero movie, Hannah would overcome these obstacles and find her way onto the field, to play the game of her life and wow the world with her skill, agility and sports IQ, making the right pass at the right moment. We would be the extras in the crowd, screaming with joy and cheering her on.

But this was not a movie. It was just the tail end of a corporate gender-diversity consultation session, and I was sure every key decision had already been made before the day had even begun. I knew what they were doing. They needed to say they'd consulted the trans community, but they didn't have to take anything we'd said on board. I was sure that we'd all been duped, paid off in ancient grain salads and mini muffins.

* * *

A fortnight later, I sat waiting for the train at Middle Footscray Station, breathing out vapour like a dragon while looking through my work emails. In between new client enquiries, I noticed with excitement that I'd received an offer of free tickets to an AFL elimination final. I texted Gemma to see if she wanted to go. The Bulldogs had sadly not made the finals, but Gemma was still keen to witness the drama of two Victorian teams slugging it out. I was ambivalent, pulled in two directions by my enthusiasm for free stuff and my disquiet about being a transgender sell-out. Gemma countered by suggesting that we sneak in a big pink, blue and white #LetHerPlay banner and unfurl it mid-game for maximum impact.

When the train arrived, I nabbed a corner to stand in and flicked over to Twitter. Scott Morrison, our brand-new prime minister, had taken offence at some signage in the toilets at his new workplace. The sign read, 'PM&C is committed to staff inclusion and diversity. Please use the bathroom that best fits your gender identity.' Morrison had gone on commercial radio to say that it was evidence of over-the-top political correctness – much to the delight of many right-wing journalists.

It was hard to believe that any of this was the top order of business for a new PM. His comments spurred a fresh wave of online debate about trans inclusion, however, which perhaps was the point.

I was glad to have work to distract myself. Unfortunately, my first meeting of the day was not with a client but with Greta, a monitoring and evaluation expert who specialised in 'nimble' projects, AKA the poor end of the market. It was a condition of our grant that we conduct an evaluation, and so I'd chosen her pretty much at random from a list I'd been given. Greta had short, curly black hair, and I couldn't tell if she was a queer woman or a trendy heterosexual from Thornbury. I supposed it didn't really matter, but it would have been good to offer this project to a member of the LGBTIQ community. I reminded myself, though, that it would literally be discrimination to not award someone a contract just because they were straight.

Greta spent the morning bombarding me with terminology I was not familiar with, such as 'theory of change', 'key performance indicators', 'targets', 'baselines' and 'data sources'. It all sounded very neoliberal and not very community. Greta then showed me a template for the communication plan and stakeholder-engagement strategy that I'd need to create.

'Is this not all a bit superfluous, given that I'm the only person working on the project?' I asked.

'But what if you get hit by a bus? Your manager will need to know where the project is at,' she replied.

I was surprised by how much project administration I was going to have to do on top of my casework. Wasn't it obvious that providing free legal help to people who wanted it would be useful to them?

Because we only had $5000 for an evaluation, which apparently was a pitiful amount, Greta wouldn't be able to provide me with her usual high level of support. As our conversations continued, it dawned on me that Greta was only agreeing to facilitate a 'project visioning day' and then give me with some Word documents that I could use as templates to conduct my own evaluation.

'So, it won't be much of an evaluation, then, will it?' I asked.

'How so?' Greta said.

'If I am evaluating my own service, it's not going to be very independent.'

'Well, the budget is very constrained.'

I spent the rest of the day setting up a SurveyMonkey to send to clients after closing a casework file or providing one-off advice. I knew that seeking honest feedback from distressed, disadvantaged people who I would probably not be able to help as much I'd like to was going to do nothing for my self-esteem. But I could also see that the feedback would be vital in providing an evidence basis for our applications for future government funding.

It was the reputation of the service that was on my mind when I asked Gemma to pull the plug on her banner-making. What if we did appear on TV? I was meant to projecting a sensible lawyerly image. What if someone from the AFL made trouble for the Queer Legal Service? I didn't think a public stoush with a major sports code would assist us when it came time to go back to government to ask for more money to keep the service going.

* * *

That evening, feeling like a rat, it only felt right when I got completely saturated in a freak downpour walking from Jolimont Station to the MCG. The rain had not deterred the vendors outside the stadium, who cried, 'Record! Get your record!' in a sing-song voice, as boys in blocky trainers and tight sweatpants crowded into undercover areas to munch on sausage rolls and pies before the game. I was getting to the stage where people were often unsure if I was a man or a woman, and I didn't feel comfortable using either toilet in a crowded place like this. So, feeling guilty, I slipped into one of the few unisex, disability-access toilets to try to dry myself off under a hand dryer. Gemma, who'd managed to stay dry, stood out the front to make sure that no one using a wheelchair needed to use the rest room.

Now drier, I was feeling much more upbeat when we met at the gates and made our way to an exclusive section on level two. We weaved past wealthy middle-aged men looking ridiculous in short-sleeved AFL guernseys worn over pressed white shirts. Neither of us had ever been in such a fancy part of the stadium before. I was served immediately by one of the many staff at the multiple bars, and then had my first frothy sip of Carlton Draft of the night. As we found our seats, Gemma pointed out all manner of celebrities, from former players to prime-time chefs to members of the Victorian state cabinet. Nearly face blind, I could hardly tell my own clients apart, so I just had to take her word for it. As we watched the first bounce, I couldn't believe how good the view was compared to up in the cheap seats. I could see every detail, right down to the expressions on the players' faces. It was like watching a completely different game. I was particularly impressed by how skilled the svelte umpires were at running backwards.

At half-time, I decided to level up on my gender-affirmation journey by going into the men's toilets. Rows of dudes stood pissing at the urinals, reminding me of footage of industrial-scale farms where hundreds of cows were simultaneously milked by gleaming steel machines. I snuck into one of the free stalls. The seat glistened with frothy yellow piss, and a previous occupant had apparently tried to flush a can of Mother down the toilet bowl. *Why were men like this?*

Gemma and I then headed back towards the bar, where we spotted Scott Morrison himself, foolishly wearing both a Richmond and a Hawthorn scarf. He was looking around with a big smile like the cat that got the cream, now that he was Australia's man of the hour. I instinctively looked away, but Gemma had other ideas. She marched up as close to him as she could. The PM looked right back at her, ready to receive her good wishes.

'You're gross,' she said.

For a moment, before returning to his usual smug grin, he looked genuinely crestfallen. We hurried off to the bar, laughing our heads off. I was certain that at any minute we'd get a quiet tap on the shoulder by a security guard and be asked to leave without a fuss. But when we got our drinks without any issues, I felt a little bolder. As we returned to our seats, we were still laughing. Gemma was a lot braver than me. I felt proud to be sitting beside her.

Chapter 5
Lesbian Body Count

One of the greatest perks of transitioning was no longer getting periods. When I happened to notice someone else's packet of pads or tampons, I felt elated. Not my problem anymore! No more accidental spillage, stained underwear or bed sheets. No more cycling emotions or tying a shirt around my waist. No more cramps, nausea or pain. Until the pain came back. I'd read on the trans masc Facebook group that these 'phantom periods', which for me often came in the early hours of the morning, were a common side effect of taking testosterone. When I met the new doctor at Equinox Trans Health Clinic, she asked me if I had any concerns I wanted to discuss.

'Well, there's the pelvic pain I'm getting,' I replied.

Reluctantly, I accepted a referral for an ultrasound. I didn't want to do it, but I didn't want to die of ovarian cancer either.

A fortnight later, I was in the fuchsia waiting room of a women's clinic in East Melbourne, feeling awkward. I was told to drink plenty of water, so I sat drinking glasses of water from the comically small disposable cups next to the bubbler.

It reminded me of the place where I'd once done a round of IVF to start a family with my partner at the time. The two fertilised eggs that a gynaecological surgeon had skilfully retrieved from my body outlived the relationship and were still in deep-freeze storage at a private hospital down the road. I'd turned my back on the technologically assisted procreation, a right that had only just been granted to 'socially infertile' people like me. Yet another complicated issue I didn't have the bandwidth to think through.

Instead, I read about the latest intracommunity controversy. A gay sex-on-premises venue called Wet on Wellington had started surveying everyone who came through their doors for their opinion on allowing trans men at the venue.

WE NEED YOUR HELP

Wet on Wellington has always been a welcoming, safe and inclusive place for cis males, but there is now a push for people who identify as male (trans) to be allowed entry during cis male days. Therefore, we need to understand how you feel about this to help us make the correct decision.

Question 1: Should a person who identifies as a trans man be allowed entry to Wet on Wellington during cis male–only days?

Question 2: Should a person who identifies as a trans man be post-op in order to be allowed entry to Wet on Wellington during cis male–only days?

Question 3: Would you continue to visit Wet on Wellington knowing that there is a possibility of seeing a naked pre-op trans man with:

Female breasts? Yes/No

Female genitals? Yes/No

Thank you for your participation.

I knew this was one of those moments where I shouldn't read the comments. But I couldn't help myself.

Gay men go to gay saunas because we are attracted to gay men and penises. I do not see how it is transphobic to not want men with vaginas in gay saunas.

Gay men go to gay saunas for penis, not vaginas. It should be no penis, no entry.

Someone else said, *Mate, it's a sauna not an A-list Hollywood orgy. You are not guaranteed that everyone in there will be to your taste, style and preference of hook-up. Not into trans guys? Great, don't f*ck one. You're being big babies.*

Another replied, *Trans men are men? Okay. Let them go to a male-only venue and see how many would line up to lick their vag in the glory holes. Delusional.*

The next comment read, *As a gay trans man, I can say from experience that plenty of cis gay men do have interest in our community, so you're just projecting your transphobic feelings and general disgust at our bodies. Cheers for that.*

The final comment I read was, *Harbour City Bears is Australia's largest association (900+) representing the Bear community and their admirers. We are an inclusive association who extends our membership to all of our siblings in the LGBTIQ community and beyond. We enjoy trans representation across our association and call on Wet on Wellington to model the same inclusiveness and respect that we have. To that end, we have donated $1000 to Transgender Victoria to apologise for the hurt caused by the gay male community.*

That was nice.

'Sam?' a young doctor with an auburn bob called out.

I followed her in. She seemed nervous and uncomfortable. I tried to tell myself I was just projecting. Fortunately, my ability to disassociate from my body came in handy. *Do what you like down there. I'm not really here anyway.*

She got me up on the table and snapped on some white rubber gloves. As she tried to use her magical wand to see my insides, my mind severed itself from my flesh. I imagined that I was dead, and that this was the beginning of one of Scully's forensic pathology scenes in *The X-Files*. Unfortunately, Scully determined that I hadn't yet had enough liquid to make my organs visible, so I was sent back out to the waiting room to keep drinking.

After I'd downed a few more cups, the doctor tried again. This time, the screen lit up with a visualisation of my uterus, cervix, vagina, fallopian tubes and ovaries. There it was, living proof of my latent womanhood.

'It all looks fine to me,' she said.

* * *

Later, a little kid was skipping around out the front of the café I was trying to enter on St Kilda Rd. I smiled at the kid's mother in an attempt to communicate that far from being annoyed, I found their child's joie de vivre charming.

'Billy, move out of the way of the nice lady,' she said to her child.

I flash of anger overtook me. *'Nice lady?' What the fuck? Who calls a person that?* Seething rage exploded from within me. I could suddenly imagine myself as the Hulk, tearing through my clothes and going on a rampage. But outwardly, I didn't react. I just smiled and stood in line at the café, trying to move my attention towards choosing between an eggplant and bocconcini panini and a pumpkin, pine nut and feta scroll. I took a few deep breaths. I knew she wasn't trying to offend me and probably wouldn't even remember our interaction in an hour from now. But my anger had taken on a new quality since starting on the testosterone. Whether it was a genuine side effect, a placebo or a psychological effect of finally permitting myself to do something I'd wanted for a long time, I didn't know. But as suddenly as it came, my fury ebbed away. Instead, I felt decisive. I ordered the eggplant panini, and decided I was going the whole hog.

* * *

After a couple of months of being on the full dose of T, my voice started to break. Increasingly, I felt that I was officially no longer part of the lesbian community. I tried to remember exactly what my life had been like as a lesbian, as I felt that world slipping away. Childhood had been a daily nightmare of fights about dresses, appropriate playmates and haircuts. In primary school I was called a 'tomboy'. By early high school I'd been renamed 'carpet muncher', before I'd even grown my own pubic hair. It was my appearance and behaviour that got me this name, not sexual activity. I'd been told I was a lesbian so many times, and the boys were so mean to me, that there seemed to be no alternative.

The boys at school were so routinely vile to me for not looking girlish that I lived my life on high alert, trying to anticipate where the next insult or can of Coke to the head would come from. Lesbian role models in the media were few and far between. There was k.d lang on *Video Hits*, crooning over long-lost lovers with an intensity that made me squirm. Ellen DeGeneres, the world's most famous soft butch, had a beige sitcom about shenanigans at a bookshop café. It was widely beloved until she came out as gay and was then dropped by her TV network. It was a very clear message: don't ask, don't tell. I wondered how many of these psychic wounds would stay with me once my surgery scars had healed?

When I finished high school, I spent my holidays before uni lost in movies. I caught a train and a bus to Planet Video on Beaufort Street in Mount Lawley, where I systematically rented every film in the 'Festival' section. I wasn't sure if this was a euphemism for gay and lesbian culture, but it sure seemed to be. I watched *Go Fish*, an arty black-and-white film about a group of butches in 1990s Chicago. I then got through *Gia*, *But I'm a Cheerleader*, *Boys Don't Cry* and *Bound*. But my favourite was *The Naked Civil Servant*, based on the memoir by Quentin Crisp, about a flaming, out homosexual in London in the 1930s and 1940s. I connected deeply with the voice of this melancholy, acerbic dandy.

The first lesbian who made a huge impression on me in real life was Del. On my first day at Curtin Art School, Del strode past in a three-piece pinstripe suit and a fedora in the blazing Perth summer sun. She was much older than me, almost thirty. I couldn't tell if I was attracted to or repulsed by her. She was a proper full butch. Hair cut short like a man's. Tall, thick and solid. Her younger brother Christopher was in my year. They were from Kalgoorlie, and he was gay too. *Two gays in one family? Their parents must've been devastated*, I thought. Christopher introduced me to The Smiths, Dusty Springfield and The Court Hotel, Perth's only gay bar.

Del was frosty and superior, just like I imagined a real artist to be. She used proper carpenter's tools to build strange mechanical contraptions that were displayed in dusty warehouse galleries in Fremantle. She didn't seem to care that my classmates made fun of her for thinking she was a man, despite her soft face and hands. I became her pest, asking her about the dense cultural theory books she had under her arms. I read the same books after she returned them, not understanding a word. From Del and Christopher, I learnt about post-modernism and queer theory and that gender was a performance. I read articles deconstructing the iconic image of Cindy Crawford, in a black bathing suit, straddling and shaving k.d. lang.

Once when I came back from the library, I found my art locker stuffed with flyers for a drag kings night at the Court Hotel. I couldn't believe it. Was I being homophobically bullied at an art school? Even in Perth, this seemed pretty out there. It turned out, though, that it had been Del.

'I thought you might want to enter,' she said, with a sassy grin.

'Why would I want to do that?' I shot back.

Being butch was a sensitive topic for me. I didn't see how I could claim the title since I couldn't drive without panicking, didn't know how to mow the lawn or fix things. I was terrified of money and bills, weak and bookish, more like a nerdy gay boy than an archetypal butch like Del. On the other hand, in my Vinnie's corduroy trousers and loose, baggy t-shirts, I was the opposite of glamorous. I was about as fashionable as a hessian sack. Did that make me butch?

'Well, maybe we can go one night anyway,' said Del.

It suddenly occurred to me, as improbable though it seemed, that Del might be flirting with me.

Del and Christopher led me and a group of fellow art students out on an excursion to the Court Hotel the following week. I'd hoped that I'd meet someone debonair like Quentin Crisp, funny, erudite and deadpan. But there was no one like him there at the gay bars, just drunk male clones who made misogynistic jokes about Del and me 'smelling like fish'. People romanticise gay bars, but they weren't very friendly. I didn't much like The Court, but the straight bars seemed even worse.

Del and I circled each other for a year or so before we made out one night in the women's toilets after a big night of booze, pool and cigarettes. Del's girlfriend Melissa, a middle-aged security guard with biceps and spiky, blonde-tipped hair, was immediately alerted by the lesbian grapevine. I was warned in no uncertain terms not to speak to her girlfriend again.

I was heartbroken. I lay in my bedroom, in a ramshackle share house in Northbridge, bawling my eyes out, wondering if I'd ever find anyone who understood me. At the end of the year, I decided to get out of Perth already.

I was in love with Melbourne from the day I arrived. It felt like I could be anything I wanted. I lived right near the Brotherhood of St Laurence, so I could buy a whole new wardrobe of winter clothes for $30. We lived on Nicholson Street, Brunswick East, in a house we named the 'Slanty Shanty', nestled next to a men's halfway house and an Indian takeaway shop. I became ensconced in a queer sub-culture in Melbourne where I could largely be myself. I joined a particular social milieu, the queer anti-capitalist left. They said that everyone should identify as queer to reject the compulsory heterosexuality. I dated a communist who was smarter and better-looking than me. These were my glory days, though I didn't know it then – lining up out the front of Q&A at The Builders Arms on a Thursday night in 2004, with all the other sloppy, drunken butches in skinny black jeans, chequered shirts and day-glo jackets. Back then, I was relatively skinny and could easily mash my small breasts down in a tight black Bonds singlet from the kids' section of Kmart to maintain a reasonably flat chest. I was supporting myself by working cash in hand for $9.50 an hour at a remainder bookshop on Elizabeth Street to top up my student Centrelink payments. To keep costs down, friends and I each took turns to smuggle goon into pubs, which we'd surreptitiously decant into used, foamy beer glasses left by other patrons. We'd then drink wine by the cupful with a Marlboro Light in hand, its red ember ready to singe friends' shirts as we robot danced to Bloc Party.

At the end of my first year in Melbourne, I received a small grant from the student union to attend Queer Collaborations, a queer student conference in Brisbane. My mind was blown. In Melbourne, universities pay for you to be gay?

A friend and I caught the hop-on hop-off bus up so we could sightsee along the east coast, which I'd never visited before. We walked wide-eyed up and down Oxford Street in Sydney, staring at drag queens, and ate choc-dipped fruits at the Big Banana in Coffs Harbour.

When we finally made it to the Queer Collaborations in Brisbane, I was exposed to concepts that I'd never come across before. People talked about ethical non-monogamy and domestic violence in gay and lesbian relationships. It was here that I first heard a radical feminist say all men are capable of rape, and likely would if given the chance. The revolutionary socialists said that transgender people were unfortunates so twisted by gender and sexual oppression that they took to mutilating themselves. Come the revolution, people like them would be free to be as butch or as camp as they liked, no longer needing to cut off their breasts or genitals.

There were other pointed debates. Feminism versus socialism. Socialism versus Aboriginal sovereignty. Gay marriage activists versus marriage abolitionists. I was immersed in all of it. Most of it was just idle talk in pubs and warehouse parties. I was not the centre of attention; I wasn't the most persuasive speaker or the bravest activist. I was just a lesbian with dirty glasses that were always getting fogged up, watching and listening.

When I got back, I was introduced to *Stone Butch Blues* by Leslie Feinberg, by my ex-girlfriend's girlfriend. The book captured Feinberg's experiences as a butch, working-class lesbian working in a factory in Buffalo, New York, who witnesses Stonewall-era police raids and eventually decides to start transitioning. The book was long out of print, and the ageing, tear-stained copy that I'd been given had been passed between many share houses in Melbourne's inner north, where it was revered as a cultural touchstone, a reminder of how difficult life used to be for queers like us.

I then met a mature-aged student called Darius in the queer room at La Trobe. Darius was a courteous, soft-spoken, short man with clipped blonde hair, who was always dressed impeccably in a tailored suit and small black shiny business shoes, which made him stand out from the rest of the students in sloppy hoodies and sneakers. Darius also wasn't like the other young men in the queer collective, who spoke excitedly about picking up guys at The Peel in Collingwood and The Market in South Yarra. Darius seemed to have a very sedate, homely lifestyle.

It took me months to clock that Darius was transgender, despite him having told me that he was studying for his PhD in transgender speech pathology.

Darius had smiled graciously at me as I asked embarrassing, intrusive questions about whether he had to get testosterone from gym junkies on the black market. He told me that the doctors at the Carlton Clinic would prescribe it, and that he'd actually just moved in with another trans man, which was convenient because they could administer each other's testosterone injections into their buttocks. Darius invited me to the launch of *Dude Magazine*, a new zine about trans guys. As I walked in and gazed around at the audience, I was suddenly over- whelmed by the sense that I really had no idea who was transgender and who was just butch.

Within a year, three of my formerly butch lesbian friends had transitioned. There was Orbs, who'd gone from being read as a foul- mouthed tattooed butch outsider to a friendly, knockabout lad from the country. There was Wren, who'd transformed from a pixyish waif to a Chapel Street twink. Koda evolved from lesbian separatist to a much-loved top in the bear scene. Lea DeLaria, the iconic butch who plays Big Boo in *Orange Is the New Black*, made headlines after she expressed her anxiety about butch erasure. I felt this too. I was happy that they were each doing what they wanted to, but I couldn't help wondering what this meant for my community. Could all of them really have been trans this whole time? Would there be any butches left in a decade? Someone had to hold the line, and I intended for that someone to be me.

But over the years I developed a secret addiction to trans memoirs. Quality was not a prerequisite. I read them all. I started with *The Making of a Man: Notes on Transsexuality* by Maxim Februari, a Dutch legal philosopher. It was an off-white hardcover book, a very expensive international import with sharp, weighty pages. *People in The Netherlands must really care about books*, I thought. I couldn't just walk up to the counter and buy it on its own, so I paired it with a Helen Garner book about a disgruntled dad who killed his kids.

I hoped the shop assistant would think I just had an academic interest in gender. I rushed home with my contraband, eager to tear open the brown paper bag.

Once I'd had my first drop, I wanted more of these forbidden, sacred texts. I soon realised that there were many more books written by trans women. I kept searching the internet until I found an 'FTM' booklist on Goodreads. Thumbnails of memoirs emblazoned with the authors' serious faces appeared: *Becoming a Visible Man* by Jamison Green, *Transition: The Story of How I Became a Man* by Chaz Bono and *The Testosterone Files: My Hormonal and Social Transformation from Female to Male* by Max Valerio.

I couldn't find any of them in bookshops, so I ordered them on eBay from the US. When they arrived in the mail, the well-thumbed paperbacks smelt like old mothballs. *Someone has been here before*, I thought. A travelling gospel. These were the kinds of books that you definitely didn't want to read in public. I didn't want to reveal my secret thoughts to anyone, especially not some random public transport passenger. It took me a decade after reading *Stone Butch Blues* to find the courage to transition. By that time, I felt the world had already shifted around me. I was running very, very late.

Chapter 6
Sing for Your Supper

It was a freezing cold Melbourne winter, and the Yarraville house, with all its cracks, felt practically glacial. Daylight savings had long ended, and the morning gloom made it a slog to get out of bed. I woke up one day with a scratchy throat, like I was coming down with a cold. A parched, croaky voice came from my lips as I said to Gemma, 'Good morning.' We were both a bit stunned. The tone and timbre of my voice had dropped overnight. The vibrations in my throat felt unfamiliar and alien. While this was something I'd badly wanted, I still found it unnerving that it was actually happening. The timing was unfortunate, too, as Polina had booked me in to give a verbal report that morning to an anonymous donor, who'd provided an extra $50,000 to top up my wages and to pay for the administrative costs of the Queer Legal Service. I'd only just found out that such a person existed, after Polina had called me the previous Friday to inform me that the donor would like to meet me for an 'informal catch-up'. I was immediately suspicious. Was I in trouble? Had they heard me on the radio and decided that their money might be better spent elsewhere?

When I got to St Kilda Legal Service, I was feeling paranoid and withdrawn, certain that everyone was going to ask me a million questions about my voice. I nonetheless did the rounds, speaking in the highest pitch I could to Sandie, Henry and the law student volunteers who staffed our telephone line. I was talking to Henry about his day in the Magistrate's Court assisting sex-worker clients on the loiter list when Polina's voice rang out from her tiny office.

'Sam, what's going on with your voice? You sound sick,' she said.

Oh god. I guessed I couldn't put it off any longer.

'Do you have a minute? I asked, shutting the door.

'Oh, leave it open, it's so stuffy in here.'

'Yeah, but it's, like, private,' I said.

She relented.

'So, the reason my voice is different is because I am taking masculinising hormones,' I said.

Polina looked at me blankly.

'Like, as in I am transitioning,' I said. 'Gender transitioning.'

'Oh, right. Right. Sorry, I had no idea. Why didn't you say anything about this before?' she asked.

'I guess, it's a bit of an awkward discussion to have,' I replied.

'Well, how long are you going to have this … issue with your voice?' Polina asked.

'I don't know. At least a few weeks, I guess.'

'Is there something we should be doing as a workplace to support you with this?'

'Well, I am planning on having chest surgery at some point. Getting time off for that would be good.'

'How long?'

'Two weeks?'

'I'll need to talk to the board about that. Is there anything else you need to tell me?'

'Nothing I can think of right now,' I said.

I'd done it. I felt so proud of myself. When I was back at my desk, I put my headphones on. I wished I could go home now. I felt utterly exhausted by the encounter. Instead, I sent Polina a copy of the guide to supporting employees while they're transitioning that my union had put together, and then got back onto my client work.

Soon it was time to walk to the café with Polina to meet our anonymous funder. I didn't even know what their name was yet, so I wasn't sure what to expect. Would it be a rich closeted gay celebrity?

'So, can you tell me who we're meeting?' I asked Polina.

'Her name's Meliora. She's an impact investor with ties to the law.'

'So, she's not, like, particularly interested in LGBTIQ issues?'

'No, I don't think so. We told her where we were putting the funding this year and she seemed reasonably happy with that.'

How many similar meetings did this woman have every week? What a life, going around being a social justice fairy godmother.

We sat down at a fancy patisserie on Carlisle Street. Five minutes later two women arrived. One pushed a pram while the other was holding a gigantic bouquet of sunflowers.

'Leah, can you take Asher, please? I'll be done in twenty minutes.'

The au pair smiled and walked off with the baby. I guessed it would be a quick presentation, then.

'Sorry I'm late. A girlfriend just gave them to me. Aren't they gorgeous?' said Meliora, putting the sunflowers on the table.

I looked at them with concealed revulsion. I hated sunflowers. Anything with a pattern of small holes and bumps brought on a wave of disgust in me. I wasn't sure that I'd be able to look at them all day. But what could I do? I couldn't believe I now had to pitch to a sunflower.

Despite the wafting smell of freshly baked croissants, Meliora took her time explaining to the waiter how to prepare her preferred liquid lunch of an apple, celery and spinach juice. During this exchange, I surreptitiously examined Meliora and her elegant, soft, tasteful clothing. I'd never met anyone who was properly rich like this before. She looked much like everyone else, I supposed, but with a glow of health and wellness that I couldn't quite put my finger on. Was it her skin or her hair? The juice? I wondered if she'd had cosmetic surgery. She didn't look a day over twenty-five. However old she was, she could buy and sell me ten times over.

I ordered an English breakfast tea and delivered the presentation in my croaky, uncertain voice. I provided an overview of the service, with the number of clients we'd seen and what kinds of legal problems they were presenting with. I peppered her with harrowing stories about the people I'd already assisted, from a queer Iraqi seeking help with an asylum claim to a young bi guy dealing with revenge porn.

I was effusive about how well things were going at Pink Panther, omitting to mention that Neil and Gryn, who were on the project steering committee, had failed to turn up to our first two meetings. Instead, I told her about how wonderful our new Queer Legal Service volunteers were, and how excited they were to have found an inclusive work placement. I felt like a dancing monkey, spinning tales of woe to shore up my own pay packet.

Throughout the presentation, Meliora nodded politely as she sipped her juice. She didn't seem especially fussed about the details.

Eventually she said, 'I'm so glad you are doing such good work and that I've been able to help.'

Polina then turned to Meliora. 'Should we discuss that other matter now?' Polina asked.

Meliora nodded, and Polina told me she'd meet me back at the office.

I stood up and left, eager to get away from the strange situation and the gigantic sunflowers.

I was starving by the time I left the café and its delicious-smelling pastries, so I grabbed a takeaway bagel down the street and ate it alone in a nearby park before walking back to the office.

When I got there, I spotted Sandie out the front chatting to Tanya, a charismatic, intermittently homeless woman who came in now and then for a food package or help with parking fines. Sandie had made Tanya a cup of tea and had just fished a red sequined blouse out of a box of clothes in the back of her car.

'Look, Tanya, you'd look nice in this. No way I'm going to wear a skimpy little thing like this at my age,' she said, laughing.

Tanya danced around, holding it in front of her, and gave Sandie a hug. 'Thanks, love, this is really special.'

Just then, Polina appeared from around the corner. She did not look pleased.

Sandie turned to Tanya. 'I'd better get back to work. Drop in again soon, love,' she said, handing me Tanya's empty mug. 'Can you wash that, Sam? I just have to move my car.'

I nodded.

Sandie had been 'just having to move her car' every two hours every single day I'd been in the office. It turned out that this was just Sandie's standard way of doing things. She was always running late and then parking in a two-hour spot, so she kept having to leave the office to move it.

'Good chance for me to have a cheeky cigarette break,' she'd once told me with a grin.

* * *

I was soon invited to come down to Happy Days in South Yarra, a drop-in centre for people who were HIV-positive, which had been running since the early 1990s. I loved being there from day one. The regulars were mainly gay men in their fifties and sixties who'd lived through the AIDS epidemic. Many of them had had rough lives. It was unpretentious, kind-hearted and community-centred. Happy Days ran a cooked lunch twice a week, which volunteers served from a steaming hot silver bain-marie. For three dollars, you could get a lamb roast with roasted vegies and mint sauce with a tumbler of Coke on the side. I started visiting whenever I could to ask if anyone needed any help, often over the jaunty sounds of a volunteer playing show tunes on a beaten-up grand piano. I wasn't much of a social net-worker, but word got around that I could help people with their legal problems. Soon, I had opened multiple files for men from Happy Days. I loved this kind of work, fighting the good fight for the downtrodden. I felt like I could've been in a similar situation to a lot of the people I worked with, but for a few lucky breaks. I got a lot of joy getting other people's lives in order, especially at a time when I didn't particularly want to dwell on my own.

One of my clients from Happy Days was called Robbie, who had been sent a debt letter by Centrelink for $18,000. Almost five years earlier, he'd received Newstart while working casually as a cleaner at a TAB in South Melbourne for a few months.

'Now, I have done a lot of stupid shit in my lifetime, love. Lots. But I seriously don't think I did this,' said Robbie. 'I'd been on the waiting list for five years before I got offered the flat in Emerald Hill. I was like clockwork reporting my fortnightly earnings. I was desperate to keep a roof over my head.'

I nodded sympathetically, while taking him in. He was wearing jeans, scuffed white sneakers and a grey hoodie, and had greying, light blonde hair. His face was pale, thin and weathered. Robbie was missing a couple of front teeth, while the rest were a motley array of yellow, black and brown. He was the kind of guy you wouldn't be surprised to see sitting on a milkcrate out the front of a supermarket, asking for change.

I had no trouble believing him. My own unexpected Centrelink debt letter had arrived in my MyGov inbox two years earlier, just after I'd started working for Legal Aid. I was terrified that I'd be prosecuted and have to declare a criminal conviction for fraud, which would probably get me disbarred. I'd immediately paid the $1200 debt, two-thirds of my fortnightly pay. It was infuriating. Three months later my mum, who worked casually at a nursing home, got a debt letter too. That's when I started thinking it was fishy. I could believe that I might've made a mistake reporting my income, but not my mum, who was honest to a fault. I'd then started reading articles in *The Guardian* about the automated income-averaging tools that Centrelink was using to identify alleged overpayments, which had been given the moniker 'Robodebt'. It had even been reported that there'd been a number of suicides.

'So, are you a gender non-binary person?' Robbie asked, pointing at the they/them badge on my rainbow lanyard.

My body seized up, immediately expecting a fight.

'Yeah, that's right,' I replied, in the most neutral tone I could.

'That's cool. We didn't have anything like that when I was growing up. It was just all dykes and faggots, you know?' he said.

Robbie told me about how he'd been going to Happy Days since he became HIV-positive in 1998.

'I was pretty depressed about it for a couple of years. Happy Days did everything for me. Got me home cleaning help when I was sick. Group counselling, yoga, the lot. They even got me that TAB job. Have you eaten lunch down there yet?' Robbie asked.

I shook my head.

'Come down next Tuesday, I'm volunteering in the kitchen. I'll give you an extra serve of potatoes,' Robbie said with a grin.

For the next two months I spent a small part of my week trying to track down Robbie's old pay slips. I sent a legal request to the TAB by email and post. Eventually, a guy called Gary emailed back to say he'd only just taken over as the new manager after the sale of the business, and they weren't sure where the old employee records were. I didn't have high hopes, but I emailed to check in a week later and then managed to catch Gary by phone a week after that. Once I finally managed to speak to him, the records were magically found and emailed to me that day. It was a lesson I kept learning: human contact gets results. An unwelcome truth for an introvert like me.

Once I had Robbie's pay slips, I had to sit down and really try to understand them. My fear of numbers and finances was so strong that I barely even looked at my own. Years of childhood poverty had made me deeply avoidant about anything to do with money. I tried to talk myself down. *It's just addition and subtraction – any monkey can do it.*

Once I'd created a rough table of his income, I attempted to marry up the numbers with the 400-page bundle of documents that Centrelink had provided to support its case. It was mind-numbingly tedious work going through hundreds of pages of redacted email chains, lightly photocopied printouts of Centrelink's internal accounting systems and client telephone contact records, which proved only that Robbie had called, but not what he'd said. I had no idea what it all meant. There seemed to be nothing in there that could be used to confirm or dispute Robbie's claim.

I called an old colleague at Legal Aid, who patiently talked me through what to do.

'Request a copy of their debt schedule spreadsheet. That shows how Robodebt is working in practice. The department is deliberately not including them in their evidence bundles. If you get a half decent Administrative Appeals Tribunal member, which I wouldn't bank on, they'll know what it all means. I'll send you some submissions to say during the hearing about the illegality of the scheme,' he said.

I wrote down everything he said and followed his advice to a tee. I had no idea how I'd do this job without my old colleague's support.

A couple of months later, I met Robbie down at the Administrative Appeals Tribunal. It was in yet another nondescript glass building in the CBD, this time on the south end of William Street. As I'd passed the nearby Melbourne Aquarium, I'd been gripped by a desire to walk in there and spend the day gazing up at jellyfish and seahorses, instead of arguing about debt in a stuffy government building. It was a bright, windy day and the plane trees were shedding their foul yellow pollen, which made my throat sting and my eyes water. I was in the middle of a coughing fit when I saw Robbie leaning on a loading zone parking sign, wearing a crumpled suit and tie and smoking a cigarette.

Immediately, I noticed something different about him. He looked a lot more respectable, and I didn't think it was just the suit. When he smiled and waved at me, the penny dropped. His teeth were as pearly white as those of a Hollywood heartthrob.

'Wow, Robbie, your new teeth look amazing,' I said.

'Yeah, I know, the Happy Days social worker got me all this free dental work through a scheme for HIV patients, cos it can fuck up your teeth, you know? God, they are saints, I still can't believe it. I feel a million bucks,' he said.

I was glad Robbie was feeling presentable because I sure wasn't. I'd put on a lot of weight since taking T, and my court clothes were now uncomfortably tight. My shirt was gaping at my chest, and every time I sat down I worried that the strained button on my pants was going to pop right off. I had been trying to observe this change in my body without judgement, hoping to expel the lifetime of fatphobia which pervaded my thinking. It was hard enough to do that in clothes that fit. Here, it was impossible. Worse, I was beginning to go through what I'd privately declared was my puffy-face era. My neck and jaw had widened, and I felt like my cheeks resembled a beaver's. There was something about the proportions of my changing face that was slightly off, and it was making me deeply self-conscious. I'd seen other people go through this awkward phase as they transitioned and assumed that it wouldn't be permanent. But the last thing I wanted to do was to hold myself up to scrutiny in a courtroom. I was getting to the point where I was sometimes called 'he', sometimes 'she', when I ordered a coffee or lunch, and I genuinely wasn't sure if I'd be read as a man or a woman today.

No one cares who you are or what you look like, I kept telling myself. As we entered the lobby, we passed a giant print of the Commonwealth coat of arms, featuring a kangaroo and an emu holding up a shield. The sheer size of it allowed me to notice for the first time that the armless emu wasn't actually doing much to prop the shield up and that, incredulously, the tiny hands of the kangaroo were doing all the work.

As we sat in a bland waiting room, the kind you'd find in a three-star hotel, our 1.30 p.m. hearing time came and went without our case being called. Another hour passed. Robbie when outside to smoke while I continued to anxiously scan his pay slips on my laptop, hoping to glean further meaning. At 2.30 p.m., Robbie and I were finally ushered into the tiny hearing room, which was one of twelve on that floor alone. It was divided by a long white counter with microphones installed for the purposes of the hearing transcript. I was relieved to see that Senior Member Dorn, a grey-haired woman in her late forties, was relatively informally dressed in a thick gold necklace, hoop earrings, stripey blue top and funky white glasses. I hoped that meant she wasn't one of the arch conservatives that Prime Minister Scott Morrison had allegedly been stacking the Tribunal with.

'Good afternoon, and our apologies for the delay,' Senior Member Dorn said, before beginning her introductory spiel. 'The Administrative Appeals Tribunal is independent of the original decision-maker, in this case the Department of Social Services. We take a fresh look at the facts, law and policy relating to the decision. We are also able to look at any new information not available to the original decision-maker, such as the pay slips that your legal representative has kindly provided.'

She then turned to Robbie.

'Now, Mr Pellington, I'll get you to swear yourself in. Would you prefer to make an oath or an affirmation?' she asked.

Robbie looked at me, confused.

'Are you religious?' I asked, gesturing at the copies of the Old and New Testament in front of us.

'Hell no,' Robbie replied, before immediately launching into an apology to Senior Member Dorn.

'Not a problem, Mr Pellington. Probably an affirmation, then,' she said with a chuckle.

I picked up the laminated copy of the affirmation on the table and handed it to Robbie.

'I solemnly and sincerely declare and affirm that the evidence I shall give will be the truth, the whole truth and nothing but the truth,' he stammered, stumbling a couple of times.

Senior Member Dorn thanked him before addressing to me.

'Ms Elkin, please proceed.'

I inwardly shuddered at the 'Ms'. I guessed I was a woman today, then. But it was hardly the time to be asserting my right to a non-gendered title. Instead, I took Senior Member Dorn through the unreliability of income averaging, as well as Robbie's difficult circumstances. It felt strange, talking about Robbie's ravaged liver and his experiences of family rejection while he was sitting right there next to me.

It was another two months before we received Senior Member Dorn's decision, and another week after that before Sandie managed to get one of the law student volunteers to email me a copy. When I saw the good news, I called Robbie immediately.

'Robbie, I've just seen the news. The decision has been set aside,' I said.

'What does that mean?' he asked.

'It means you won't have to pay the debt. You won! Well done,' I said.

'Thanks, love. You've been my guardian angel.'

When I got off the phone, I felt great. I had made a real difference in someone's life. These weren't the kind of cases that made for dramatic nighttime TV shows, but I didn't care. I just wanted to help people like Robbie.

Chapter 7
The Sad Stats

Sitting on a tram, on my way to run my first LGBTIQ inclusive practice training session for other community lawyers, I was completely preoccupied by the amber pus-filled pimple seeping on my back. It was so painful I felt like I'd been stabbed. Since I'd gone up to the full dose of testosterone, hormonal acne had broken out all over the middle of my back and arse. I felt fucking gross. I read the news on my phone to try to distract myself. Prime Minister Scott Morrison had just tweeted, 'We do not need "gender whisperers" in our schools. Let kids be kids.' This led to yet another wave of hysterical Murdoch newspaper commentary about trans-inclusion education initiatives having gone too far.

I thought back to my own childhood. When my parents had enrolled me in primary school in Perth in 1990, I was already a thoroughly gender-nonconforming six-year-old. I had my hair cut short and refused to wear the girls' pleated blue school skirt. The teachers didn't know what to do with me. I tried to get my classmates to call me Sam, but my teacher kept correcting them.

'Her name is Sarah and she's a girl, not a boy.'

Some of the teachers seemed to really have it in for me, for reasons I couldn't understand. When I was in Year 3, I was even made to sit at the back of the room, facing away from the blackboard, for the last two weeks of term as punishment for talking in class. I'd never seen this happen to anyone else. It was upsetting to consider how different my life would've been if my teachers had been trained to spot a potential transgender child. Let alone having access to puberty blockers and gender-affirming healthcare.

I then read about Mhelody Bruno, a Filipino trans woman who'd just been strangled to death by her Australian male sexual partner while on holiday in NSW. It was a horrible story. I briefly considered adding a reference to her killing into my presentation, but it all seemed a bit ghoulish.

I stepped off the tram at Bourke Street to enter the dingy headquarters of our peak body. I was buoyed to see so many chairs lined up, ready to be occupied by my well-meaning colleagues. On the other hand, I felt incredibly exposed. I was certain I looked like shit; I'd well and truly entered the puffy face era. The community legal sector was small, so I expected to see many old workmates at the presentation. I knew that they'd be scrutinising my appearance for signs of my changing gender, no matter what I said.

As the attendees filed in – each newly adorned with a small 'she/her' or 'he/him' handwritten pronoun sticker, hastily repurposed from the stationery cupboard – they smiled at me encouragingly while I nervously fiddled with the unfamiliar laptop. As I loaded my presentation, my co-presenter Fiona appeared at the back of the room. Fiona was perhaps the last person at Pink Panther that I would've chosen to give a training session with. Fiona ran Holding the Man, Pink Panther's men's behaviour change program. A brassy middle-aged woman with spiky blonde hair, I had assumed her to be a lesbian until I observed that she to manage to drop her husband's name and heterosexual status into daily conversation.

She was also deeply opposed to gender-neutral toilets, which was another one of her go-to topics. One afternoon while I was photocopying some documents, she asked me unprompted, 'What if a man comes into the women's toilets and assaults me during one of our men's behaviour change sessions?'

Since I'd started using the gender-neutral toilets at Pink Panther, I'd never seen anyone go into different toilets to the ones they usually would. The men continued to use the bathrooms with urinals and stalls, while the women used the ones with stalls only, despite the gender-neutral signage. As far as I'd observed, the only person who'd switched toilets was me.

'Could you use the staff-only toilets on level one, if you're worried about it?' I offered.

'Why should I have to do that? It's my workplace,' she said, before stamping off.

Before beginning, I smiled warmly at Fiona and invited her to introduce herself to the group of seated community lawyers.

Fiona took her opportunity to tell a whole new group of people that she was straight, and then we kicked off. I began by saying, 'Studies show that LGBTIQ people are more distrustful of the police, lawyers and the justice system than others. Can you think of any reasons why that might be the case?'

Then I switched to my next slide, which offered a potted history of the criminalisation of homosexuality and gender-nonconforming behaviour in Victoria since the colonisation of Australia.

- 1949 Death penalty stopped being on the books for sodomy in Victoria

- 1977 mass arrests of 'suspected homosexuals' at Black Rock Beach

- 1981 Decriminalisation of sex between men came into effect in Victoria

- 1994 Tasty nightclub raid in Melbourne

I cycled through some images to try to jazz up the presentation. A modern-day photo of Black Rock Beach, full of athletic women marching along the bay in hats and striped shirts, seemed an unlikely site for such momentous queer history. I then showed the now infamous photo of the 1994 Tasty nightclub raid, where five men had been directed by police to line up with their hands against a shimmering wall mural.

'Just after midnight, forty police officers burst into the nightclub and proceeded to strip search the predominantly gay and transgender clientele on the grounds of it being a drug bust. The searches were incredibly invasive, including cavity searches and the examination of foreskins. Some of the patrons launched a class action against Victoria Police, led by a lawyer who was there on the night of the raid. More than 200 patrons received payouts, but many more never came forward for fear of being publicly outed.'

I moved onto the next slide, which had a quote from one of the most well-known Australian High Court cases, *Green v The Queen*.

'Yeah, I killed him, but he did worse to me … He tried to root me.'
Malcolm Green, 1993.

'In this case, Malcolm Green was said to have reacted to being gently touched by his victim by punching him thirty-five times, repeatedly ramming his head against a wall, and stabbing him ten times with a pair of scissors. Controversially, the High Court found that a non-violent sexual advance could be enough to establish provocation. This is colloquially known as the "gay panic defence". It wasn't abolished in Victoria until 2005. It's still a legal defence in South Australia,' I said.

I moved onto my next slide.

'Female same-sex partners were prohibited from accessing assisted reproductive technology in Victoria until 2008, and until 2015 the *Crimes Act* included a law which singled out intentional HIV transmission for harsher penalties of up to twenty-five years imprisonment, in contrast to the twenty-year maximum penalty for manslaughter. Same-sex partners have only been allowed to adopt since 2016 and, as you all know, same-sex marriage only became legal last year. So, there's a long legacy of legal mistreatment of LGBTIQ people in Victoria that still affects the way we interact with the criminal justice and health systems.'

My audience looked appropriately vexed by these facts.

I flicked to the next slide.

'Here's some stats on the health and wellbeing of LGBTIQ people as compared to the rest of the population,' I said.

'In the last twelve months, 58 per cent of LGBTIQ Victorians have faced unfair treatment based on sexual orientation.'

'Almost a third faced verbal abuse, and 22 per cent faced harassment such as being spat at or offensive gestures. More than 10 per cent experienced sexual assault, and 43 per cent reported being in an intimate relationship where they faced abuse.'

'Rates of depression, anxiety and suicide are high. Almost one in two LGBTIQ adults have been diagnosed with anxiety or depression, compared with just over one in four non-LGBTIQ adults. More than 20 per cent have been homeless. Almost three-quarters have considered suicide, compared with 13.2 per cent of the general Australian population. And almost 10 per cent of young LGBTIQ Victorians have attempted suicide in the past twelve months.'

I thought I heard a young woman in the audience start weeping. But perhaps she was just blowing her nose.

'As you can see from these statistics, queer and trans people are unfortunately more likely to experience poor mental health and attempt suicide – not because there is something inherently wrong with us, but because of stigma, prejudice, discrimination and abuse.'

I looked at my audience, wondering if they thought that I was likely to be suicidal as well. I felt torn between the need to express a sufficiently righteous level of anger about this injustice, and my compulsion to demonstrate that I, as a fellow lawyer, could stand dispassionately in the face of unpalatable facts when required. More than anything, I felt a need to dissociate myself as an individual from *those* stats. I wanted to show my colleagues through my impromptu jokes and easy smile that while my clients and my community might be suffering, I certainly wasn't.

As I stood there with my PowerPoint, faced with an audience who were undoubtedly already well-acquainted with the more difficult aspects of the life of LGBTIQ people, I wondered whether trotting out these statistics was doing more harm than good. Was this all just serving to reinforce the link between gender and sexual diversity and mental illness?

There was something I found unsavoury about all this misery making. I wished that there was a way to plead for special rights on the basis of being particularly amazing.

I moved onto more comfortable ground, telling my clients' stories to illustrate the flaws of our legal system. I peppered my presentation with de-identified case studies to highlight the ongoing violence and distress experienced by LGBTIQ people in detention centres, psychiatric wards and prisons. I was able to draw on my own work in court to highlight the impact of rigid court etiquette on trans people: I could describe the visible embarrassment of magistrates who were unsure whether to refer to me as Mr or Ms Elkin during the early stages of my medical transition, and my endless discomfort at not being able to access a safe toilet.

I mentioned gender policing in public toilets. I tried to make it funny by telling a story from when I was working as a locum lawyer up in Darwin. Back in Melbourne my soft butch identity was generally well understood, but in Darwin I was regularly read as a fourteen-year-old boy. I went on a tourist outing one weekend to see crocodiles jumping in the Adelaide River. I had to go to the toilet before I got on the boat. The women's bathrooms were empty when I entered, but while I was washing my hands a young woman in a flowing batik dress walked in, looked confused when she saw me, and then walked back out again. She then returned a couple of seconds later seeming even more perplexed. *Here we go*, I thought. She looked back at the triangular-dress-wearing female sign on the door for final confirmation that she was the one in the right here, and then stared at me pointedly with her arms folded.

'I think you're in the wrong toilet,' she said.

'I think I'm not,' I replied in my high, female voice, before walking past her back out in the sunshine.

I said to the audience, 'That was awkward enough, but then I got stuck sitting next to her on the boat for an hour.'

I told them about watching the gigantic prehistoric-looking reptiles leap out of the water to chomp down on thick strands of buffalo meat, which the tour guide dangled off the side of the boat with a rope.

'The whole time, I was privately preoccupied with whether this woman was going to apologise to me at any point. She did not,' I said, with a laugh.

It felt important to keep things upbeat.

I was highly conscious of Fiona breathing next to me. I hoped that she wouldn't pipe up with her own thoughts on gender-neutral toilets. I suddenly felt overwhelmed by sadness and anxiety, and struggled to maintain my composure. This just seemed to make the group more keenly attentive of me. I was immensely relieved when I got to the end of my slides and Fiona took over to run her part of the session. I sat down to watch her present the definitions of lesbian, gay, bisexual, transgender, intersex, queer and asexual. I almost laughed out loud when the Gender Unicorn popped up on screen, followed by their comrade in arms, the Genderbread Person. I saw people eagerly writing notes and taking snaps of the slides. We then broke out into small groups to practise asking each other our pronouns.

I was paired up with Henry, who was dutifully sitting in the front row to support me.

'Hi Henry, I'm Sam, I use they/them pronouns. What do you use?' I said, hyper conscious of the fact that I hadn't been confident enough to introduce myself in this manner when we first met six months ago in St Kilda. I regularly felt like a hypocrite in these training sessions. I privately hated the introductory 'pronoun name around' exercise that we advocated for at the start of every meeting in these workshops. It just felt like everyone who wasn't trans got to perform their allyship, while I got to feel skin-crawlingly uncomfortable by outing myself again and again. It was a damned if you do, damned if you don't situation.

We finished by imploring everyone to take some of the LGBTIQ rights posters we'd put at the back of the room and to fill in the evaluation survey at the end of the session.

'Gotta collect those stats!' I said, trying to make a joke of the increasingly overwhelming monitoring and reporting requirements I had subjected myself to. The room tittered politely.

When we finished the presentation, I was as desperate to leave as my colleagues were keen to introduce themselves and thank me for the informative training session. I smiled and thanked them for coming, feeling more and more drained by the minute. Finally, the last of them filed back downstairs, and I was left alone with Henry, who'd stuck around to help me pack up. I asked him how things were going for him at work.

'I'm actually quitting at the end of the month,' Henry said, as he folded a chair.

'Oh no. That's too sad. Have you got another job?' I asked.

'No, not yet. I've been thinking about it for a while, but it was a bit of a spontaneous decision in the end,' he said.

Henry told me that he'd been drowning in work and had asked to drop one of his regular outreach sessions.

'Basically, Polina said no, and instead she offered me an extra job as the managing lawyer of the night service,' Henry said.

'Extra pay?' I asked.

'What do you think?' he replied.

'God. So, what do you reckon you'll do next?' I asked.

'I dunno. Sleep. Apply for jobs. Make boutique soaps,' he said.

I laughed, but then immediately apologised when I realised he was serious.

Henry showed me pictures of his swirling, multicoloured prototypes.

'I've booked in at a few makers' markets. I'll probably bomb but, you know, I just need to do something else for a while,' he said.

'Good for you, Henry,' I replied.

On my way to catch a train at Melbourne Central, I decided to reward myself by buying a razor. My transition had brought me so many new products to lust after, but I didn't have any male friends who I felt I could ask for guidance. I'd never heard men talk about things like where they bought their beard-trimming products. It was all totally mysterious to me. There were new brand names to learn about: Braun, Wahl, Panasonic, which I'd thought only made TVs. Then there were endless varieties – rotary vs. foil electric, five-in-one, single-blade shavers, waterproof. I was suddenly fascinated by all of it. Was this gender euphoria? Given that I had barely any facial hair, though, it was difficult to narrow my options based on my skin type and hair coarseness.

I lurked out the front of a shaver shop, staring at the different packaging. There were endless pickings of men grinning with snow-white shaving cream on, often coming in or out of the shower. I kept staring until I identified the most mid-range option I could find. Seemed like a good place to start.

I then peered into the shop to see who was working there. If it was a dude with a beard, there was no way I was going in. Luckily, it was a young woman. She looked like she was just out of high school, and had zero interest in her job. Perfect. I went right in, picked up the shaver I wanted and headed to the counter, terrified the girl might be replaced at any moment but an older, furrier colleague. Fortunately, it remained just the two of us. I tried to say as little as possible during our transaction. Gruff. Masculine. Barely verbal. But when she handed me my purchase with a smile, I betrayed myself by being too friendly.

'Thanks so much, have a good day,' I said in a cracking, uncertain voice.

* * *

I was looking out the window as the train rolled into South Yarra Station when I received an email from Dave.

Dear Sam,

I've attached your letter, confirming that you meet the criteria under the DSM for gender dysphoria. It can be difficult reading these letters, so please do reach out to me. I've also sent a copy to your surgeon, Dr Desmond.

I opened the attachment and briefly scanned the letter. My life story and all of its gender traumas had been turned into a series of short sentences and dot points. It ended with:

> *Through my sessions with Sam, they more than meet the criteria for persistent Gender Dysphoria (ICD-10 F64.1, DSMV 302.85, post transition). I remain happy to continue to provide review and any transitional therapy as required if Sam feels this is useful during the period ahead.*

I suddenly wondered if I had to notify the Legal Services Board about my diagnosis. Could it put into question whether I was still a 'fit and proper person' to practice law? I shut my phone and went back to looking out the window. I supposed I should feel relieved, excited or nervous. But it was all too much to take in. I just felt numb. I certainly wouldn't be dwelling on my diagnosis any further with Dave, now that I had my surgery letter.

Chapter 8
A Symbolically Binned Dick

Gemma drove me to my initial top surgery consultation at a private hospital in East St Kilda. Her car had become a lot more chaotic since we'd got together, with her make-up spilt all over the front seat and Tibby's copious black fur caked to the back seat.

This end of St Kilda was full of upmarket grocery and coffee shops, where the well-appointed locals would think nothing of dropping a hundred dollars on a quick business lunch. Orthodox Jewish schools held pride of place on huge corner blocks, lined with numerous indistinguishable late-model black SUVs for the afternoon school pick-up. It was distinctly the kind of place that most trans people could not afford to live in.

I'd googled Dr Desmond before the appointment. A photo appeared of a middle-aged white man wearing a light blue hairnet and matching scrubs. I peered at his image, wondering if he'd had some work done on his face. Did cosmetic surgeons do free little touch ups for each other throughout the day, like hairdressers seemed to?

'So, how are you feeling about all this?' Gemma asked, as she weaved expertly through the slow-moving traffic.

I'd now been on testosterone for eight months, and I'd become almost completely emotionally inarticulate. I could faintly remember the deep and meaningful conversations Gemma and I used to have. I felt as though I'd turned into a blockhead. I was sure Gemma must be disappointed. Connections with people felt less intense. Everything was now under a layer of shatterproof glass.

'Um, I don't know. Nervous?' I said.

'And how are you feeling about removing that part of your body?' she asked.

I thought about it. For thirty years I'd been uncomfortable with my small, triangular breasts. I was a chubby kid, so it felt like I'd always had them. In the last few years, I'd cycled through different styles of binders. They weren't easy to wear. The pressure on my chest just made me more conscious of my breasts than when I went around in a couple of tight singlets beneath my clothes.

'Yeah, good. Can't wait to get it over with,' I replied.

Gemma, who'd once again been blessed by the parking gods, pulled into a spot right out the front.

'How are you feeling about it?' I asked.

Gemma teared up.

'I'm happy if you're happy,' she said, as we got out of the car.

Gemma's initial response to my news that I had decided to transition had not been ideal. She'd bawled her eyes out for most of the weekend, and then told a mutual acquaintance without my permission. Since then, she'd done everything she could to support me, from attending innumerable trans performance nights to penning her own law reform submissions. I suspected that she now felt she couldn't say what was really on her mind a lot of the time, which made me sad.

'You don't have to be happy about it. It is objectively a pretty weird thing to do,' I said, trying to encourage her.

'Let me take a photo of you by the sign before we go in, so we can remember this moment,' she said.

And with that, another photo of me looking wooden with a weird expression on my face entered the digital history books.

In the trans masculine Facebook group I'd joined when I started taking testosterone, Dr Desmond – who was one of few surgeons who did the procedure in Australia and seemed to have the best reputation – had variously been described as 'fat-phobic', 'problematic' and 'weird'. I'd learnt that until recently Dr Desmond had refused to operate on anyone with a Body Mass Index (BMI) of more than thirty, due to the added potential for complications for people carrying excess body weight. While I 'liked' the comments of everyone who piled on about the racist origins of the BMI and the damaging mental health consequences of weight stigma, I anxiously calculated my own BMI in another tab.

It was 27.5, smack bang in the middle of the overweight range. I'd gained 8 kilos in eight months, and was pretty sure it wasn't muscle. I took a deep breath. I tried to take this information in without judgement. *Who cares? BMI is bunk*, I told myself. And at least it was under thirty.

I checked in at the front counter. As Gemma and I took a seat in the hallway outside Dr Desmond's office, I quickly glanced at the four other people waiting nearby. There was another trans masculine person who, like me, had brought their girlfriend for support. I read the other two as trans women who seemed not to know each other and had come separately. There seemed to be a wide array of surgery procedures on offer. There were the ones that everyone thought about, including breast augmentation, removal of the penis and scrotum and construction of a vagina and labia. But then there were all kinds of facial surgeries available to reduce the size of a trans woman's chin, jaw, nose and Adam's apple, as well as electrolysis to remove body hair and Botox injections to swell lips and soften the appearance of cheekbones.

It was almost unimaginable to believe that anyone could get rich off the trans community, but when you broke it down procedure by procedure, Dr Desmond certainly must have been. I wondered if a swapsies system would ever be developed, where trans women and trans men could swap penises for ovaries.

Gemma and I chatted and played hangman on the back of crumpled file notes while waiting for my turn. Being in a hospital was making me nervous and scared. The last time I had surgery, to fix a broken kneecap, I'd had an experience that stayed with me. As I was being wheeled in, slowly losing consciousness from the anaesthetic, I distinctly heard one of the doctors making fun of my tattooed, female body.

'Here's an interesting specimen,' he said to a colleague, before they both cracked up laughing.

It made me want to avoid another hospitalisation at all costs, so it felt strange to now be coming in of my own accord.

I went to the toilet, where I saw a sign on the back of the door by a university research team. They were seeking information from trans masculine people about their experiences receiving sexual healthcare.

I diligently scanned the QR code and began to take part in the research when I returned to the hallway. I must've already done a dozen research studies since starting testosterone.

When it was finally my turn, Dr Desmond said with a grin, 'Hey boss, come on in.'

He took me through my options: double incision method, where he would remove and later reattach the nipples, leaving a scar line under the pecs, or the circumareolar incision method, which left the nipples attached to generally maintain sensitivity, causing a high scar across the nipple line. Prioritising nipple sensation was not typical, as most trans guys just wanted to ensure that they had the most scar-free chest possible.

He got me to take off my shirt and drew lines all over me, as if I were a dead pig hanging at the back of a butcher's. He then took several photographs of my chest, while Gemma quietly snapped her own pics so that I might remember this moment forever.

Dr Desmond explained all the risks and possible complications, such as death under the general anaesthetic and the need for touch-ups down the track. He asked me if I had any questions.

I said no.

'Okay, boss, well, I'll see you in a few months. My receptionist will find you the next available date. Just remember we need your psychiatric approval letter to be dated within three months of the surgery date, otherwise we'll have to cancel,' Dr Desmond said, holding the door open for us.

The receptionist took my $500 payment for the consultation, and then checked for the next available surgery appointment, which turned out to be exactly nine months away.

'It's a very popular surgery right now,' she said, by way of apology.

* * *

That night, I had a vivid dream about my childhood friend Kara, who I hadn't thought about in decades. In the dream, she was a mad scientist cutting off my breasts, her long blonde hair getting into my wounds, causing a mess. I woke up hot and sweaty, disturbed by the dream. It didn't take me long to work out why she'd been on my mind. In Year 6, Kara was my new best friend. She was tall and athletic – I was short, dumpy and had tangled brown hair that was veering into unintentional dreadlock territory. Kara's mum saw me running around the basketball court at our first training session and decided that I needed a crop top. She instructed Kara to lend me one of hers, after I said that I didn't have one and that I didn't think my dad would pay for one.

I felt amazing the first time I put that crop top on. It was tight and cinched me up, making me entirely flat-chested. I wore it to training and then the first and only basketball game I ever played for the Wanneroo Giants. I scored two points, for the other team, when I freaked out and threw the ball up after taking a rebound on the opposition's side of the court. Kara really wanted me to keep playing, but I was too humiliated. She said that I'd have to give the crop top back if I wasn't going to play anymore. So I lied and said that I had lost it, which wasn't a smart decision since I saw Kara every day at school. I kept wearing it anyway, hoping she wouldn't notice, but she did. 'Mum said you can't come over until you give the crop top back, so give it back already, okay? I can tell that you're wearing it.'

I was cornered. I went into the girls' toilet, took it off and gave it back to her. I had been wearing it every day for months by then.

To shake off the memory of the strange dream, I got up to go to the toilet and get a glass of water. When I walked into the shared kitchen, I was surprised to see a fifty-year-old man with curly grey hair sitting at the counter, drinking a bottle of red wine on his own. Bobo seemed to know him, as he was curled up by his feet.

'Oh, hello, I'm Sissie's uncle. My sister owns the house. I was just in the area and thought I'd drop in,' he said, his teeth stained with red wine.

'Okay,' I replied, filling up a tumbler of water.

I shut the door to the kitchen and went back to bed. While Gemma slept beside me, I stewed over what had happened. I was ropeable. These fucking rich kids were treating me like an idiot, letting me pay their family's mortgage while the whole family treated the house like their own personal crash pad. But at least it had taken my mind off my upcoming surgery.

* * *

The next day, my first client was a trans woman in her early sixties
called Mona. When she'd booked in to see me, she said she wanted
to make a health complaint against the Cotter Gender Clinic, which
offered the only publicly funded trans surgeries in the country to
people who were financially disadvantaged.

'I've been on the waiting list for genital surgery for three years now,'
Mona said with a grimace.

'I've heard it can take a long time,' I replied, nodding sympathetically.

'They told me that I can't have my surgery anytime soon because
there's too many trans men and non-binary people wanting mas-
tectomies now, and they're putting them ahead of me because their
procedure is cheaper. It's not fair.'

I paused for a moment, trying to think of what to say. I didn't think
it was especially fair that I had to pay ten grand for my own surgery
either. Or that I had to sit with an impassive look on my face while
Mona complained about the rise of trans masculine 'queue jumpers'.

'Is there something specific you wanted legal help with today?' I asked.

'I want you to make them put me back to the top of the list,' she said.

'I'm sorry, but I can't do that,' I replied.

She began to cry.

'I understand that this news must be upsetting,' I continued, 'but how
they manage their waitlist is really a clinical decision for them. If
they'd taken you off the list altogether, that might be different, but —'

Mona stood up suddenly. 'I know how I can get it done if I really have to. I will just take matters into my own hands, and then make them sort it out,' she said.

She then made a gesture of cutting off her penis and throwing it in the wastebasket, as she continued to bawl her eyes out.

I asked her to sit back down and offered her a tissue. Instead, she picked up her things and stormed out. I said goodbye to her with a painted smile on my face.

As soon as she left, I collapsed back into my chair. I stared at the wastebasket, at Mona's symbolically binned dick.

* * *

Later that day, I had another dick-related appointment. Brian, a 45-year-old from Pascoe Vale, had been on his way to visit relatives in Adelaide. For reasons known only to Brian, he started masturbating in the public train carriage. He got kicked off in Dimboola and was arrested by the local police. Brian had brought to our appointment a DVD of the video interview with the police. Luckily, my Dell was so old that it still had an internal DVD player. The two of us peered down at my screen to review it.

We looked at a recording of Brian, in a knock-off Adidas tracksuit, sitting in the corner of a tiny, windowless interview room. He looked rough as guts, with bleary eyes and a five o'clock shadow. The camera caught half of the top of the two balding police officers' heads, who peppered him with questions.

'Do you agree that you exposed your erect genitalia on the V/Line train this afternoon?' one of the officers asked.

Brian slumped further down into his seat and nodded.

'I can see you nodding – can you please confirm your agreement with my statement for the purposes of the record of the interview?' the officer said.

'Yeah,' Brian said.

'Do you agree that multiple members of the public were in a position to view your genitalia when you did this?' the second officer asked.

'There was only one bloke sitting directly across from me,' Brian replied.

'Do you have anything to say as to why you did this?' the first officer asked.

Brian shrugged. 'Bored, I guess,' he said.

'Had you had anything to drink? Any alcohol?' the second officer asked.

'Nah, not for a few hours.'

'On any medication?' the first officer asked.

'Just Prozac,' Brian replied.

'Anything else?' the first officer asked.

'I had a couple of cans of Red Bull on the train,' Brian said.

I watched as the shoulders of the two officers shuddered up and down. I couldn't really hear, but it was pretty clear they were pissing themselves laughing.

Nothing else of substance was said for the rest of the recording. When it was finished, I popped the DVD back out of my laptop and handed it to Brian.

'So, were you planning on pleading guilty?' I asked.

'Do you reckon that would affect my employment?' Brian replied.

'What do you do for a living?'

'PE teacher.'

My heart sank. 'Yes, Brian, a conviction for sexual exposure is definitely going to limit your ability to teach,' I replied.

'Do you think I should plead not guilty, then?'

'Well, you've admitted to the two elements of the offence of sexual exposure, and it sounds like there is at least one eyewitness. So, yeah, I think you're unlikely to succeed with a not-guilty plea at this stage,' I said.

I gave Brian some pamphlets about Pink Panther's counselling program for alcohol and other drugs and strongly suggested he try to get an appointment with them before his next court date, so that he could show the court that he was trying to address the underlying issues that led to the offending. He seemed non-committal.

I sighed. I knew getting frustrated with Brian was not going to help either of us. Being patient with people who were unable to act in their own best interests was half the job of a decent community lawyer. But at this point, I was shit out of ideas about how to help him.

* * *

On my train home, I read a BBC article doing the rounds on the internet. Thousands of pulsating creatures resembling disembodied 10-inch pink penises had washed up on a beach in California. Twitter was alight with dick jokes: 'Ladies, if you aren't satisfied at home, remember there are plenty of fish in the sea.' I then ended up reading about a rainbow-coloured, deep-sea worm that lies in ambush on the seabed and attacks unsuspecting prey, often snapping them in half with its razor-sharp jaw. Known as *Eunice aphroditois*, scientists had nicknamed it the 'Bobbitt worm' in reference to Lorena Bobbitt, who caused a global news sensation when she cut off her husband John's penis with a carving knife in the US in 1993. It was such a big story that even I, at age ten, living on the other side of the world in Marangaroo, heard all the grisly details in the playground. Why did this cock, temporarily removed from its undistinguished American owner, end up being so very famous? What was so funny about a man without a penis?

As I changed trains at Flinders Street Station, I re-familiarised myself with the facts of the case. It turned out that the real story wasn't very funny at all. Lorena said that she'd done it after John had raped her, not for the first time in their marriage. After she cut it off, he was so drunk that he just fell asleep. Lorena drove off and threw John's penis into a field, but soon called the police to confess what she'd done. The police collected his penis and packed it in ice, and it was successfully reattached. A quote from the treating urologist, James Sehn, hit me in the guts: 'It was a kind of an out-of-body experience ... It really takes your breath away to see this kind of disfigurement.'

When I rushed onto the Williamstown train and grabbed one of the few remaining seats, an unwelcome thought hit me: *Would my body take a doctor's breath away too?*

Chapter 9
Laterally Yours

The next morning, I stood out the front of Southbank Police Station, with frigid wind pummelling my face. I was waiting for Opal, who I'd agreed to meet against my better judgement and was now kicking myself.

I'd opened a file for Opal a few months ago to help her with some public transport fines. She lived in Frankston. She was funny, artsy and a bit nerdy. In another life, she seemed like the kind of person I might've ended up in a writers' group with. I'd told her that if she needed any future help she should get in touch, thinking that it might be more fines. Instead, she'd called me in tears as I was leaving Pink Panther late on the previous Friday.

'Sam, the police want me to give a formal statement about a rape claim that's been made about me,' Opal said.

'Oh god, that sounds serious. Have they put the allegation to you?' I asked.

'Yes, it's Amelia, my ex's new girlfriend. She's told the cops that I raped her, but I haven't so much as held her hand. It's all bullshit. My flatmates have kicked me out over it already, and you won't believe who's moved in,' she said.

'Who?' I asked.

'Amelia,' Opal replied.

I was thoroughly confused.

'My ex-girlfriend, Kacey, is on the lease. Amelia's doing everything she can to steal my life. She's taken my girlfriend, she's started transitioning, and she's moved into my bedroom. And now she's trying to get me sent to jail,' Opal said, through tears.

'So, Amelia is a trans woman too?' I asked.

'Yes, we're all trans,' Opal replied.

Fuck, I thought to myself. I could only imagine how the police were going to deal with a rape allegation against a trans woman by a trans woman.

'So can you meet me?' Opal asked.

'You really need a criminal lawyer for something like this,' I said.

'But I trust you. You get it, you're trans too. I just want to go and clear my name. Honestly, there's nothing in it.'

I'd tried to dress as male as possible in an effort not to confuse the police. I wanted to cross over, make things as easy as possible. I'd decided that a preppy, clean-cut look without my glasses was the easiest way to pass; for some reason my glasses seemed to push me back into the butch lesbian category. The only time I consistently didn't pass was when I was with non-binary people or lesbians – then my gender was rendered suspect by association. What was I going to look like standing next to Opal, though?

I checked my emails while I waited, and noticed I'd just received one from Dave.

Dear Sam,

I hope you're well. I have a quick request.

I wanted to see if you might be interested in presenting to the Victorian Mental Health Royal Commission, as a transgender mental health consumer who has been a client with our service.

Regards,

Dave

I knew exactly what Dave was referring to because I was working on the Queer Legal Service's submission to the royal commission. I watched as a police car pulled into a 'No Parking' spot. Opal came around the corner in a furry orange jacket and white Converse sneakers. I put my phone back in my pocket.

'Sorry I'm late, my train was delayed,' Opal said.

'No problem,' I replied.

We entered the police station together. No one was staffing the front desk, unless you counted Constable T. Bear, a Public Order Response Team–themed grey teddy bear kitted out in a helmet, fluoro vest, riot shield, gun, baton and protective knee pads. Apparently, I could purchase my own Constable T. Bear, from a whole range of different uniforms, from the Blue Ribbon Foundation for just $65. I wondered if they came with their own secret recording devices.

I looked up at the CCTV in the corner and waved to try to get someone's attention in the back area. I saw myself in the circular mirror in the corner of the room. I was at my most androgynous yet. I had a matching pimple on either side of my chin, as though I was about to grow a pair of elephant tusks. I felt ugly, huge and tiny all at the same time. The last thing I wanted was to be in a police station, observed by unseen police officers. I wondered what they were doing behind the door. Were they looking at us and laughing?

We took a seat. There were signs for family violence support programs, missing persons signs and a dog-eared Reconciliation Week poster from a few years ago.

I looked down at my shoes, which were many sizes smaller than Opal's. I was endlessly self-conscious about how small they were.

Opal had been told to come in by nine a.m. to meet with the Frankston Sexual Offences and Child Abuse Investigation Team. An hour later, two detectives walked through the front door, holding two steaming McCafé coffees. One was a woman with stylish tortoiseshell glasses and long brown hair captured in a high top-knot bun. The second detective was a tall barrel-chested man with a shaved head.

'Sorry to keep you waiting, traffic was terrible. Come on through,' the female detective said.

Opal and I followed them to a small, windowless room with a one-way mirror, instantly reminding me of my time at the transgender speech clinic. We went over some preliminary details, before the female detective put the allegation to Opal.

'It's alleged that on 17 March 2017, while engaging in kissing and cuddling with Ms Amelia Garson, you then inserted your penis into the victim's anus without consent.'

'That never happened. I've never ever been in bed with Amelia,' said Opal, mascara-stained tears running down her cheeks.

'So you deny raping Ms Amelia Garson by inserting your penis into her anus without her consent?'

'I do.'

The two detectives looked at each other. I couldn't tell what was going to happen next. Were they going to arrest Opal? I was terrified for her.

'Now, um, this is obviously a bit of a sensitive topic,' said the female detective, 'but we've been doing some reading and, uh, we've read that oestrogen depletes the ability of a person with a penis to develop and maintain an erection. Is that the case for you?'

I had suggested to Opal that she might give a 'no comment' interview, but it now dawned on me that they were feeding her lines to help her case. It seemed like they'd already made up their minds not to continue with the prosecution, but I had no idea why.

'Yes, that part of my body doesn't, um, become erect anymore,' Opal said.

The detectives wrote down some notes. They asked a few more questions to confirm the dates that she'd moved in and out of the property. Ten minutes later, the interview was over. When we got out of the police station, Opal began to cry.

'Can I give you a hug?' she asked me. 'Thank you so much for being there for me.'

I said yes, even though I don't even hug my own friends most of the time. The situation seemed to warrant it.

I walked off, feeling emotionally wiped. Of course, I had no way of knowing what had really happened between Opal and Amelia. I wasn't sure what to make of the police's line of questioning. When I started at the Queer Legal Service, I hadn't considered the possibility of representing one trans client against another. It made me feel weird.

Over lunch, I went back to my email from Dave and wondered what to do. I knew that royal commissions were a very particular kind of theatre called by governments to inquire into matters deemed to be of public importance. In the previous few years, it had felt like there were multiple going on simultaneously, and their significance, form and value were as variable as their nebulous titles suggested. Some felt monumental, such as the Royal Commission into Institutional Responses to Child Sexual Abuse, which provided survivors of sexual abuse in the churches an opportunity to tell their truth to a powerful government appointee, and which saw some of the most influential people in the world sit down for cross-examination. Some felt more forced, such as the banking royal commission, which came about only after one too many rorts twisted the federal government's arm. Whether politicians went on to implement the recommendations was a whole other question.

I knew I was way too busy to take this on. But, on the other hand, who else was going to do it? How many other trans people would have the confidence to get up and give evidence to a packed royal commission?

So, despite my reservations, I dashed off a quick reply to Dave saying that I'd be happy to help.

* * *

Later that day I met Pedal, who was nineteen and newly out in the trans community. Pedal had been invited by an older trans woman called Gloria to come and stay at her place in Brisbane, where they had sex a few times. A week later, Gloria started making allegations on social media that Pedal had sexually assaulted her. Pedal's social media feed was suddenly full of public comments and private messages from other trans people, telling them that they were scum for what they'd supposedly done, and that they weren't welcome at community events. Pedal, who denied the sexual assault, intentionally overdosed and ended up in a psychiatric unit. When they got out, they were linked up with a queer family violence service called Helping Hands, which sent them my way.

'Has Gloria gone to the police?' I asked Pedal.

They shook their head. 'I don't think she'd do that. Gloria hates the cops.'

'Okay. So, what is it that you're most concerned about?' I asked.

'I just want everyone to stop messaging me. They've even started messaging my high school friends, encouraging them to unfollow and block me. I feel like I can't get away from it all,' Pedal said.

'Do you know who these people are?'

'I only know them online. I don't know their legal names or where they live or anything,' Pedal said.

This made things difficult. I didn't think the law could help Pedal with this problem.

'Could you go offline for a while?' I asked.

Pedal began tearing up. 'But how would I talk to anyone?'

I didn't really know what to say. Mainly to make myself feel better, I printed for Pedal some fairly useless fact sheets about personal safety intervention orders and how to report abuse to the eSafety commissioner. I told Pedal to call me if they were contacted by the police, and then left it at that.

I found cases like Pedal's both depressing and confounding. It was starting to dawn on me that a lot of the queer community's wounds were self-inflicted. It seemed that we unleashed our fear, anger and frustration on each other because we felt powerless to confront the institutions that actually held us back. Still worse, it seemed like the people passing on unchallenged gossip and publicly shaming others genuinely thought they were doing the right thing. But for the person it was happening to, because the pile-on was coming from within, it led to a heightened sense of betrayal. I didn't like the tendency to label people 'problematic' and then leave them in purgatory forever.

It offended my core sense of justice. Once you had that label, there seemed to be no clear path to move on from what had happened. It was the kind of punishment that could make an already marginalised person lose hope.

While all of this drama continued, the Queer Legal Service would never be short of work. Being exposed to these stories from my clients made me even more wary of trans online spaces. I didn't like the tinge of a sanctimonious mob mentality and was terrified of expressing my own opinion, lest it somehow upset the wrong person and lead to a cascade of criticism from all corners of the internet. If we couldn't make room for nuanced discussions or forgiveness for breaches of the ever-changing protocols around language and theories of gender, how would we create a supportive community at all?

It seemed much safer to find a sense of kinship amongst the long dead. I became fascinated by the life of proto trans man Edward De Lacy Evans, a nineteenth-century Irish immigrant who lived and worked as a male in the Victorian Goldfields for two decades before being sent to Kew Asylum, where they were revealed to be female-bodied. Evans was labelled a 'male impersonator' in his day, a term I quite liked. I had to laugh when I imagined the blowback I'd receive if I began adopting this term to describe myself.

* * *

A week later, I was off to my meeting with some lawyers working on the royal commission. I struggled to find the right office, which was in an outdated building next to a food court and a touristy chocolate shop in the middle of Collins Street.

I had to call a mobile number to be brought up to the office, which clearly had been hastily assembled after the government surprised everyone by announcing the terms of reference months ahead of schedule.

I was greeted by Debbie, the mental health support worker, a kindly, slightly teary-eyed woman in a large, knitted jumper; Richard, a personal injury lawyer with a short, trendy haircut; and Claudia, the QC who would be leading the evidence in court, an impressive woman in her forties with a high ponytail and expensive casual business attire.

I knew exactly what they wanted: a sob story about how the mental health system had failed to provide me with care when I needed it most, due to a lack of services, not enough competent practitioners, long waiting lists and red tape. I knew I had those experiences in abundance, so while Claudia went through her spiel about how they 'take statements from many, many more people' than they are able to use and that they'd 'need to carefully consider' whether they'd ask me to give evidence in the hearings in the coming weeks, I smiled, knowing full well that they would choose me. Not only did I have the stories, but I was a trained courtroom advocate. They wouldn't have to worry about me falling apart on the stand when it was time for me to get up and give evidence.

I started telling my stories. A hospital admission to ED after punching my arm through a window, which ended in a nurse telling me I was 'a very silly girl' and that sick people needed the bed I was in. Calling the work-funded employee assistance line only to be told they didn't deal with 'trans issues'. Unanswered calls to mental health crisis lines. I saw Claudia shift to a more interested posture and nod faintly at Richard, who doubled down on his efforts to create comprehensive notes on his Surface Pro.

I felt uncomfortable telling an intelligent and accomplished QC about all of my personal difficulties, with one of my contemporaries writing it all down. Richard was doing the exact kind of job that I did; there was a chance that we might sit next to each other waiting for the same job interview one day. Claudia had the kind of distinguished career that I could aspire to but would probably never reach, especially if I kept blurring the line between my professional mask and the murkier truths of my own interior life. But like so many that came before me, I wasn't immune to the pleasure that came from receiving the approval of an authority figure for giving them the exact story that they wanted. I peered over at Richard, who was typing away. It was uncanny watching him as a client rather than as a colleague. We were in sync, the three lawyers, with me speaking in crisp sentences that Richard could easily put into chronological and thematic paragraphs. Debbie broke the legal bubble by entering the room after a ten-minute hunt to find a box of tissues I hadn't asked for. She seemed pleased with herself, having found such a precious resource in this barren wasteland of an office.

When we finally finished, I checked my voicemails. I'd missed an urgent call from a highly distressed trans woman who'd tearfully said that she was being held in solitary confinement in the psychiatric wing of the women's prison. I suddenly felt very ashamed. My own tales of woe paled by comparison, and that mine wasn't the story that really needed telling.

Chapter 10
Religious Freedom

I was on my way to Victorian Trades Hall, which was hosting a panel about religious freedom. I walked past the austere bluestone remnants of the Old Melbourne Gaol, where Ned Kelly was hanged. I then passed the Eight-Hour Day monument. The tall, granite column was reminiscent of a thin, grey penis with a jaunty golden bauble on top. I'd spent half my life going in and out of Trades Hall to attend everything from activist meetings to drunken discos to late-night comedy shows. The last time I'd been there, it was for a frenetic street party to celebrate marriage equality. Since then, the Australian Christian Lobby and its allies had been campaigning for extra protections against what they saw as dangerous sexual and gender ideologies. Of critical importance to the religious freedom campaigners was their right to sack non-adherents from religious schools and to refuse to provide medical treatment where it conflicted with their beliefs. They construed LGBTIQ rights as a runaway freight train that was going to destroy their way of life.

When I reached the imposing neoclassical building, I felt myself to be a bit player in the ongoing story of political Melbourne. I entered the main meeting room and waved to Holly from Helping Hands, the queer family violence service that was hosting the event.

'You're the first panellist to arrive – take a seat up here,' Holly said, ushering me to a long wooden table at the front of the high-ceilinged room.

A handful of audience members were already waiting. I recognised a few of them from the AFL gender diversity consultation. My appearance had changed a lot since then, and I was passing most of the time now. Although I enjoyed passing as a man, I still felt incredibly ugly and self-conscious. I was sure that everyone was scrutinising me, to see how my body and face had morphed and expanded from the testosterone. I kept reminding myself that it wasn't a beauty contest, and that I was here to talk about an important issue. I noticed Dave, my gender counsellor, sitting on his own at the back of the room. I hadn't gone back to see him after he sent my surgery letter. *God*, I thought, *he's probably writing a research report on transgenders in the wild.*

Florence from Rainbow Rights strode in next, with all the confidence and gravitas of a future prime minister. Rainbow Rights was one of several national LGBTIQ campaign organisations currently in a messaging battle to claim that they had 'won' marriage equality. I found the whole thing very distasteful. Florence barely acknowledged me and took the seat furthest away, spending the few minutes before the forum started tapping out emails on her iPad. Next, a guy called Kenny with a long white goatee from the Uniting Church showed up, who mercifully sat in between Florence and me.

The room was full by the time Holly introduced us and gave the audience a short overview of the Religious Discrimination Bill. She then threw to Florence, who began with a slick PowerPoint presentation.

'We've got to be smart if we want to defeat the bill. That's why we're undertaking a series of private, "inside track" discussions with politicians from across the spectrum to try to build opposition in Canberra to the changes,' Florence said, before ending with a QR code for people to donate to Rainbow Rights.

Next up, Kenny spoke about how much his progressive church supported the LGBTIQ community. He suggested that everyone in the audience sit down and have a cup of tea with at least three people to discuss the issue in a respectful, non-confrontational way. While Kenny seemed nice enough, I'd been raised to be wary of Christians.

My parents were atheists, and I'd grown up on stories of my Yorkshire granny being beaten by the Catholic nuns at her school. I could still hear her constant refrain that Catholic priests loved nothing more than to 'diddle' young boys behind the church pews. Since her views had been at least somewhat confirmed by the global investigations into institutional sex abuse by the Catholic Church, my desire to stay as far away from the church as possible had only strengthened.

Then it was my turn. I hadn't come prepared with a speech, so spoke off the cuff as best I could. I explained that I'd turned eighteen a month after 9/11, coming of age at the beginning of the so-called 'War on Terror'.

'So, having lived through the ugly rise of Islamophobia that engulfed the Western world, I understand the importance of defending religious freedom. But I think we've already got the balance right.'

I then explained a couple of Victorian civil law cases that demonstrated this.

'In a 2014 case known as Cobaw, Christian Youth Camps, a company associated with the Christian Brethren religion, operated the Phillip Island Adventure Resort. Cobaw – a community health organisation that ran Way Out, a youth suicide prevention program for same-sex attracted people living in rural Victoria – tried to make a booking at the resort. When the worker at Cobaw told the manager of Christian Youth Camps about Way Out's stance on homosexuality and their plan to have workshops and discussions over the weekend to raise awareness, the manager suggested she look elsewhere to make a booking.

'Cobaw took the matter to the human rights tribunal. Christian Youth Camps argued that they didn't discriminate, but that if they did, they were entitled to under the religious exemptions in the *Equal Opportunity Act*. The Victorian Court of Appeal ultimately found that Christian Youth Camps did discriminate because the religious exemptions didn't apply. This was because they found that there was no specific tenet of the Christian Brethren religion that stipulated they avoid contact with people who do not share their religious beliefs, nor that they had to avoid contact with same-sex attracted people who do not share their religious beliefs, nor that they were required to openly express their disapproval of same-sex attraction when in contact with same-sex attracted people.'

I looked around the room. I felt like I was losing the audience. It was hard to explain the nuances of discrimination law in a way that was interesting to the layperson. That's why it was so strange that the ins and outs of this previously niche area of law was being discussed daily on the national stage.

'There was also the Bendigo mosque case. A few years back, the Bendigo Council received over two hundred objections to a purpose-built mosque being constructed in the area. The matter went to VCAT, where the opposers essentially argued that an Islamic mosque was an intrinsically unacceptable use of land because of the very nature of Islam, which they said would create social disharmony. VCAT rejected this argument, and the mosque was built. So, this shows that our current laws are already getting the balance right to protect religious freedom.'

I signalled to Holly that I was finished, and she sprang up to take questions and comments from the audience. The first person was a woman in her twenties, who introduced herself as a committee member from an anti-racism collective. 'What you have said tonight is all well and good, but why are there no people of colour on this panel?' she asked. 'The media are already pushing a narrative that it is people of colour who are most opposed to LGBTIQ rights in Australia. Why are you adding to this by only having white people on stage?'

Holly stood up to apologise for the oversight, mentioning a last-minute cancellation of a fourth speaker.

'Well, it's not the Muslims, Hindus or Sikhs pushing the Religious Freedom Bill,' the woman continued, 'it's the hard-right white Christians that have taken hold of the Liberal Party. Now that they have Scott

Morrison the evangelist as their leader, things look dire for us. Perhaps you might consider actually working with other minority groups to oppose the legislation,' she said.

She then went on to outline some possible unintended consequences of the bill, such as creating an atmosphere that would enable intra-religious sectarian conflict in Australian workforces, enabling a scenario where a Hindu manager could say disparaging things to a Sikh junior staffer about their Sikh faith with impunity.

She definitely should've been on the panel.

'What about people with disabilities?' another audience member said. 'A lot of religious people believe that children with disabilities and even mental illness are a punishment from God. What happens if a nurse says this to a vulnerable young mother who's just given birth to a child with a disability? Imagine the consequences.'

We on the panel nodded along and said, yes, yes, this could all be possible. The crowd was beginning to look petrified.

When the forum came to an end, I couldn't bear the thought of sticking around for the next steps planning session. I'd already done a full day of work, and after expending my remaining emotional energy on stage, I felt totally drained. When it was announced that it would be governed by consensus decision-making, which I found inefficient and tedious, that made up my mind. I was out. My neck and back were killing me.

* * *

I went to see a physiotherapist the next day. When I was on the table, I thought about how in a few months I'd have large scars across my chest, which would forever mark me as trans in any health appointment when I had to take my top off. I imagined someone looking at my body and then asking me to leave. It wasn't a nice prospect.

131

The physiotherapist told me I was extremely tense. *No shit*, I thought.

Gemma had asked me to switch from the daily cream to testosterone injections because she was worried that her moustache was getting darker, and that I must somehow be accidentally getting my T on her. I joked that this was probably because she'd just turned thirty, but I agreed to it in any case.

So, after I was done at the physio, I went to get my first testosterone injection down at Equinox Trans Health Clinic. But when I arrived, the receptionist was incredibly apologetic.

'I'm so sorry, but our nurse has actually gone home sick, and we don't have anyone else who can do injections here today,' they said.

'Could Dr Levi do it?' I asked.

'Dr Levi isn't with Equinox anymore, unfortunately. We've got a new doctor starting in a fortnight,' they said.

I sighed. Everything to do with trans stuff was run on the smell of an oily rag, and everyone always seemed to be quitting. I tried to book in at a community health centre in Footscray to see if I could get my injections done there. The first appointment was a week away. When I finally saw a doctor there, he seemed horrified about what I was asking him to do.

'Isn't there a specialist you go to see for this sort of thing?' the doctor said.

I explained that my doctor at Equinox had left, but there were a lot of fact sheets on their website about how to prescribe testosterone. He told me he didn't have time to look into it, and that I'd have to get my file sent over, and maybe we could talk about it at my next appointment. And with that, I was dismissed.

So, running out of alternatives, I asked my friend Fabian, who was a non-binary medicine student, if they'd come round to administer it. I felt a bit weird asking Fabian because we'd previously had long conversations about them possibly beginning hormones, and they'd even tried my testosterone cream a couple of times. They ultimately decided they didn't want to keep taking it, because they wanted to retain their flawless skin and soft hair. I didn't want them to feel like I was shoving trans stuff down their throat. As it turned out, they were more than happy to do it, and confirmed that they were confident to administer the intramuscular injection. I dropped round at Fabian's after work one day and lay on their bed with my pants down, as they prepared the biggest syringe they could find.

'God, look at your arse, it's getting so hairy,' Fabian said with a laugh.

I was sure that my pimply, furry behind would practically be an advertisement against taking testosterone. I felt a momentary shock as the wide needle entered my body and thick, viscous fluid flowed into my bloodstream. Despite the pain, it was an unexpectedly euphoric experience.

* * *

For the next few months, I wrote submission after submission to the seemingly never-ending series of reviews and enquiries launched by the federal government into religious freedom, peppering them with depressing hypothetical scenarios:

- a pharmacist refusing to fill a trans client's hormone prescription due to their religious beliefs;

- a nurse refusing to give a patient information about how to access a late-term abortion in a public hospital due to their religious beliefs;

- a psychologist telling a lesbian client that her lifestyle is sinful and that's why she is depressed.

I was sure that none of this was any good for my mental health.

On the weekend, Gemma and I decided to drive down to Walkerville in South Gippsland to get away from it all. A Legal Aid colleague, had given us a standing invite to stay in her and her partner's unoccupied '80s pop top caravan which was parked on a bush block down there. They'd installed a double bed, lighting, a stove and a microwave oven in there themselves. Even though I was personally uninterested in DIY projects, I was very grateful we had such handy, generous friends. We went down a winding road to the secluded beach at Walkerville South, where we were met with pristine white sand, historical lime kilns, rock pools and spectacular views of the nearby national park at Wilsons Promontory. After a swim in the icy Bass Strait, we soon dried off in the hot sun as I got to indulge in my favourite activity, reading on the beach. I took out my copy of Carlo Levi's *Christ Stopped at Eboli*, a 1930s memoir of an Italian doctor's experiences in political exile in a remote region of southern Italy. I'd packed it because it had absolutely nothing to do with queer or trans culture, which I wanted a break from. But when Levi recounted meeting a gravedigger with a 'sexless' voice, prominent breastbone and absent beard, I was intrigued. Had I just come across yet another proto-trans character where I least expected to find one? Or was I seeing things that weren't really there? As the sun began to set, we went back to the caravan and cooked steaks under the stars on a beaten-up, old camping stove. We then climbed into bed. The mattress sagged in the middle, and Gemma and I laughed as we kept rolling onto each other. We were both terrified about the prospect of spiders crawling on us in the night, so we ended up sleeping right next to each other, like tin soldiers, to avoid the walls as best we could.

The next morning, Gemma cooked a delicious shakshuka on the outdoor stove while I brewed the billy tea. Tibby, Gemma and I then headed down a bush track to the beach at Walkerville North, past wombat burrows and masses of tea-tree. I was wearing sneakers that were one size too big for me in an effort to hide the petite size of my feet. Between the too-large shoes and Tibby pulling on her lead, desperate to get to the water, I managed to trip on a rock and fall down a hill. My right leg ached, and Gemma had to help me limp down the narrow path to the secluded beach below. Once we made it, Gemma took off to find help, as I sat on the beach, throwing a stick to Tibby to keep her occupied. I felt embarrassed and depressed, and increasingly worried that if a calamity befell Gemma, we'd both die out here alone on the shore. Eventually, my anxiety levels dipped and I was able to relax a little, despite the throbbing pain in my legs. I enjoyed the feeling of the gritty white sand underneath my feet and the crashing sound of waves. *It's nice here*, I thought. Growing up in Perth, I'd felt like a freak at the beach. I just couldn't fit in with the relentlessly heterosexual, image-conscious surf culture. There was less of that in Melbourne, probably because the bayside beaches were as still as backyard swimming pools. I noticed that in the distance some kids had made a giant dick and balls sandcastle, featuring seaweed ball hair and a thick, veiny schlong. It was quite artistic. The wind started to whip up sand, which flew at my face. I looked over at the big doodle. It too was under attack from the wind. I lay down to protect my face and was just nodding off when Gemma came back with a young guy called Jim, who worked at the fish and chip shop at the caravan park. Jim drove us all the way back to our car, while regaling Gemma and me with stories about life in the caravan park. I loved meeting considerate young men. It didn't happen very often.

When we were back in Melbourne, my GP sent me for an X-ray of my knee. The place was in Moonee Ponds, a grungy, well-used building. I'd changed my Medicare ID over to male, which turned out to be remarkably easy. So, when I checked in, they called me Mr Elkin. I didn't realise they were going to scan my whole body – I went right into the machine. When I got out, I could hear the staff sounding confused.

'Um, so you should have told us you might be pregnant,' one technician said, an uncomfortable look on his face.

'Oh, there's no way I could be pregnant,' I replied.

'Still, you should have told us. We need to put a lead apron over women to protect their reproductive organs,' he said.

I felt embarrassed after being chastised. It seemed that I was going to have to pre-emptively out myself anytime I had any sort of medical procedure, even when it had nothing to do with my genitals. I would never be free of being transgender.

Chapter 11
It's the Most Wonderful Time of the Year

We were edging towards Christmas, my least favourite time of the year. Going home at this time was a complicated prospect for pretty much every LGBTIQ person I knew. Along with the financial strain of buying thoughtful gifts and fancy food, there was the added emotional pressure of playing happy families with people who weren't especially supportive. Dodging homophobic relatives at boozy events was tricky, not to mention habitual misgendering from even the most well-intentioned. No matter what I did, I always found Christmas a painful reminder of my lack of family connection. For those who didn't celebrate, the cultural baggage was still difficult to avoid. It was also the busiest time for community lawyers, who regularly saw a spike in family violence, parenting disputes, mental health admissions and drug- and alcohol-related charges in the lead-up to the 'happiest day of the year'. The transferred stress exacerbated my bad habit of rubbing the tip of my thumb across my dry, split cuticles throughout the day. By the end of the week, I had little ragged bits of torn skin below the nail fold, which occasionally spilt streaks of blood onto my file notes.

I had no intention of going back to Perth to see my family for Christmas. The year before, in the fog of brand-new love, I'd decided to ask Gemma to travel 3500 kilometres over to WA with me to visit my complicated family for Christmas. When we'd arrived at my brother's place in Northam with my mum smack bang on midday, I was shocked to find they'd already eaten without us. My brother's wife had gone to bed, and my niece and nephew were nowhere to be seen. Gemma and I sat down with a plate of leftovers. My dad was his usual obnoxious self, droning on about his latest hobbies and adventures in Asia with his new wife and child, without asking Gemma or me a single question about ourselves. But when he made a particularly disparaging comment about my mum, I asked Gemma to come with me on a walk.

As we stood on the suspension bridge over the Avon River, looking out at the tranquil rich-blue water below the cloudless sky, I turned to Gemma.

'I'm so sorry I brought you here. I'm never coming back.'

This wasn't the first time I'd promised myself never to return. But when we got home, I stopped making any effort to stay in touch with my dad or my brother. They either didn't notice or didn't care. I had no intention of telling either of them about my transition. But Mum was more difficult. I felt I had to tell her about my upcoming surgery, but couldn't imagine ever managing to do so.

In mid-December, I saw on social media that a young trans woman called Bridget Flack, who was a local DJ and poet, had gone missing. Her friends feared for her life. Glitchy footage of her entering and exiting a Collingwood bottle shop played over and over again on a loop on the news. The police were reluctant to allocate the resources to conduct a comprehensive search, and so a request went out through the various trans groups for volunteers to search the Kew wetlands near where she'd last been seen. Fabian and I spent the early new year trudging around bushy creek beds, looking for her. Every time I saw anything human-made amongst the scrub, I was terrified that we were about to stumble across her body. We walked around for hours, but only found old cans and empty chip packets. Two days later, the news came through that another group of volunteers had found the body. I was relieved it wasn't us.

* * *

A couple of days later, I received an invitation from Holly to attend a queer orphans Christmas breakfast she was organising for Helping Hands. The email invite said:

This time of year can be hard on many in LGBTIQA+ communities. We're inviting LGBTIQA+ folk and allies to a morning of great food, a makers' market and entertainment.

I thought it might be good for me to be around other queers who struggled with complicated family situations, so I asked Gemma if we could drop in there before heading up to Leongatha in Gippsland for lunch at her nonna's place.

Flagstaff Gardens was right in the middle of the legal precinct, and thus not a place I associated with relaxing, good times. I tried to keep an open mind. When Gemma and I arrived, there were about thirty people sitting around on colourful beanbags in front of a giant inflatable rainbow, which people were taking selfies in front of. A buxom drag queen called Frock Hudson was onstage dressed as a sexy Santa, lip-syncing to Mariah Carey's 'All I Want for Christmas Is You'. We went to get some food, where Holly and her colleagues were serving up egg and 'facon' rolls with chutney. We walked around looking at embroidered patches, friendship bracelets and resin pendants, before spotting a boutique soap stand. The sign hanging off the table said, 'Handsome Henry's'.

I skipped up to Henry's stand, where he and his partner were selling fragrant soap in all the colours of the rainbow, decorated with imitation fruits, bow ties and candies.

'Henry, how are you?' I asked, giving him a pat on the shoulder.

'Great! How are you, Sam?' he asked.

'Oh, you know, it's the same as usual, so feeling pretty stressed. I'm so glad to see that you got your soap-making business going,' I said.

Gemma and I bought some Cherry Ripe–themed soaps to give to her family, and then headed over to find some spare beanbags to watch the show. We were offered a Christmas cracker by a volunteer. We tugged on it and I won the prize, which was a crispy red paper crown and a fake nose, which I put on in an attempt to be jolly.

Moments later, a familiar face walked past me. It was Mona, the trans woman who had got upset with me a few weeks ago for not helping her get to the top of the Cotter Gender Clinic waiting list. Either she didn't recognise me or she didn't want to talk. I suddenly wondered how many more of my clients were here. I kept my fake nose on.

The next performer was Ze/zir salad, a non-binary slam poet dressed head to toe in fronds from an actual Christmas tree. Multicoloured baubles hung from their limbs and their face was painted as a gold star, dripping with tears. Ze proceeded to indulge the crowd with an arguably too long, non-rhyming poem about topping Jesus with an 8-inch pink strap-on. After listening politely for the first five minutes, Gemma went to find a drink, while I quietly slipped my headphones on and checked Instagram. In the last couple of months, I'd started receiving a flurry of spam messages from fake accounts of scantily clad women. It felt like a milestone. Somehow, I'd crossed over the gender lines in the eyes of social media. I passed almost all the time in public now, but how on earth did the algorithm know that?

Gemma brought me back a non-alcoholic sparkling wine and we cheered to our relationship, as the Victorian Commissioner of LGBTIQ Communities took to the stage. Like me, they had been a butch-of-centre queer woman who'd recently started using gender-neutral pronouns. They were the first person ever appointed to the role, which was created by the Andrews government. It was slightly unclear to me exactly what the role of the LGBTIQ Commissioner was, but they certainly knew how to give a speech.

The crowd gave hearty applause as they came onto the stage. They were in their fifties, wearing a purple shirt with grey pants and a daggy dad tie of Santa catching a wave.

'This year, friends, after we survived the punishing marriage equality campaign, and continue to be subjected to harmful public rhetoric from the debates around so-called religious freedom, I wanted to reflect on mutual respect and compassion.'

The Commissioner went on to make an impassioned plea for members of the LGBTIQ community to support each other, and not get sucked into in-fighting. At this point Mona, who was sitting on a pink beanbag at the back of the crowd, interrupted their speech.

'You're nothing but a dog! You do nothing for us, you just take your big fat pay checks and let us suffer! You'll get your comeuppance.'

The volunteer with the Christmas crackers hurried over to Mona and led her away from the group, as tears poured out of her.

We all turned back to the Commissioner. How would they save this?

'Well ... what can I say? Merry Christmas, everyone,' they said, before handing back the mic.

I watched them head towards their parked car. I was certain I'd be on the receiving end of similar treatment soon enough. It felt like it would just take one vocal disgruntled former client to permanently sink my reputation.

Gemma and I said our goodbyes and went back to her car. As usual, Gemma drove while I played co-pilot, putting on Sia's new Christmas album to Gemma's approval. As we speed down the M1, headed for South Gippsland, I kept Gemma entertained by reading out some of the latest dramas I'd observed on queer social media. In my trans masc Facebook group, someone called Kai was calling out another member for being 'truscum'.

'What's that mean?' Gemma asked.

'Dunno,' I replied.

I searched online for a definition: (*slang, usually derogatory*) *A person who believes that gender dysphoria is an essential trait to being transgender. Synonyms: transmedicalist, transmed. Antonym: tucute (slang).*

'I thought that gender dysphoria was kind of a given?' Gemma said.

'Me too,' I replied.

This led me down an online rabbit hole. On one side, people were arguing that those who have no intention of medically transitioning but insist others respect their increasingly bizarre neopronouns – such as xe/xem, zir/zem and shark/sharkself – were discrediting the 'real' transgender rights movement, which would inevitably lead to a backlash. On the other, people said that trans people shouldn't be policing each other's language and choices, and that they are just projecting their internalised transphobia and bigotry onto younger trans people who are creating a whole new way of doing gender. I felt at sea in these cultural debates. The way I saw it, declaring myself to be non-binary as opposed to a trans man or even a 'man of trans experience' did not feel like an especially important distinction. No matter what I called myself, I'd still be a person with female primary sex characteristics who'd taken hormones to acquire a masculine appearance. The current discussions about identity were steeped in the neoliberal individualism of our age, marked by a conception of the world that I found deeply anti-collective. Surely my identity was not a question that I could solely answer myself, but was something thrust upon me by other members of society? This was exactly the kind of thought I would never post online. I didn't want to be publicly shamed for being the wrong kind of trans person.

I could see all kinds of heated debates raging everywhere. Over on Instagram, a prominent queer woman was calling out a cisgender, gay male for 'taking up too much space' in their nascent LGBTIQ refugee rights activist group.

And on Twitter, a white non-binary writer was being called out for having publicly disclosed on Transgender Day of Remembrance their experience of sexual violence, because some felt that the day should be exclusively used to expose the global epidemic of violence against trans women of colour.

When I read a post by a trans guy shit-posting about a new trans health service, suggesting that everyone boycott it because of their 'problematic' intake forms, my amygdala was officially in overdrive. I put down my phone and tried to focus on the rolling green hills of South Gippsland for a while.

After arriving at Gemma's nonna's house, we were welcomed warmly and invited to sit at a full table of friends and relatives. Gemma's family were loud, retelling old stories that had entered the family folklore, as her Nonna Connie offered us endless servings of cotoletta, polpetta and lasagne. Here, I could finally tune out from all the online drama, and instead listen to stories about feuding distant relatives and the latest fruiterer news. In the late afternoon, we drank short blacks and sat around watching an online feed from a webcam on Stromboli, the volcanic Aeolian island that Connie and her sibling had chain migrated from in the early 1950s. We then moved on to the family's bizarre annual festival tradition of measuring each other's freakishly large heads.

When it got to five p.m., I decided that I really needed to call my mum. We usually spoke on the phone at least once a fortnight, but since my voice had deepened from the testosterone, I'd felt more and more uncomfortable about calling her. Every time we spoke, she was convinced I had a cold. Sometimes I fudged the truth and agreed that I'd been a little under the weather. But now that I had my chest surgery booked in, I felt guilty about not explaining what I was doing. The lies left me on edge, feeling duplicitous and ashamed of my cowardice. What did I even care what she thought? I was long past thirty now, surely far enough away from childhood to be worrying so much about what my mother thought about my life choices?

I poured myself a glass of red wine and stepped into another room to make the call. It would be just after two p.m. in WA.

'Hi, Mum,' I said.

'You still sound sick,' she replied. 'Have you got the flu?'

'Yeah, no ... Actually, the reason my voice sounds strange is because I am taking, uh, masculinising hormones. To, you know, appear male in public. I just think I'll be more comfortable that way,' I said.

My heart was like a bomb going off in my chest. What was she going to say?

'Oh,' she replied.

Silence followed.

'Yeah, so I, uh ... thought I should just let you know,' I said, mainly to fill the dead air.

I waited for her to reply for so long that I thought the Telstra signal had dropped out in her area again. I took another sip.

'So does that mean you'll be getting a penis stitched on?' she asked.

I was so shocked that she went straight to the genitals that I almost dropped my glass.

'Um, no, no, that's a bit out of my price range. But I am getting chest surgery to remove my ... my breasts,' I said.

'Is that dangerous?' she asked.

'No, not really, it's just an overnight procedure,' I replied.

'It that expensive?' she asked.

'Yeah. It's like $10,000.'

'I just spent another $200 taking that stray tom to the vet to pop his latest abscess from fighting. You wouldn't believe the smell. Putrid. Anyway, he's sitting having a good sleep on the armchair now,' she said.

I took this segue as a cue that we were done talking about my transition. I wasn't expecting much in the way of emotional or practical support. I was just incredibly relieved that I'd managed to spit the words out.

Chapter 12
Administrative Violence

On the last weekend before returning to work in the new year, Gemma and I were relaxing at our favourite Seddon café when we read that neo-fascists were planning an anti-immigration march along St Kilda Beach later that morning. Neither of us felt like it, but confronting a gathering of actual Neo-Nazis in Melbourne felt mandatory. There, for the first time in our lives, we witnessed a large mob of men in tight polos and streetwear openly performing the Sieg Heil as they marched along the beachfront. I thought of the Nazi youth who looted the Institute of Sexology in Berlin in 1933, setting fire to irreplaceable research about transgender people's experiences. I was sure that if we let the Neo-Nazis congregate now instead of running them out of town, they'd be coming for us next. But there weren't anywhere near enough counter-demonstrators there to outnumber them, and it was only the huge contingent of mounted police that kept us from being attacked. When the rally began to peter out, we headed back to our car. Just outside Luna Park, a group of Neo-Nazis spotted Gemma and me in our 'No Room for Racism' t-shirts. They started shouting and running towards us. We jumped in the car and took off in terror. Things were starting to feel apocalyptic.

* * *

Back at St Kilda Legal Service, Sandie had just been made redundant. When I walked in, I could see that she'd been crying. The vibe in the office between Sandie and Polina was tense, and I rued the fact that my desk was in between theirs. I put my headphones on and started wading through all of the new referrals that had amassed over my new year break.

I had a bunch of unanswered voicemails from Daniel, a gay man from Moorabbin who'd taken out an interim intervention order on Boxing Day against his now-ex partner Wayne. I felt guilty for having been on leave while he needed help, so I called Daniel to find out what was happening. I spent an hour on the phone with him, explaining how to end a lease early on the grounds of family violence and commiserating about his brand-new three-seater white leather sofa, which had suffered multiple wine spills during Wayne's unauthorised new year's party. When I hung up, I decided to re-record my telephone message, since my voice had changed so much over the last year. I listened back to tentative sounds of my girlish ghost voice. This auditory reminder of my former self was profoundly unsettling, but I still felt terribly guilty when I deleted it. It was as though I'd drowned a beloved sister. I then started looking through a bunch of letters I'd received from transgender prisoners during my time off. Months ago, I'd put an advert about our service in a free newsletter for LGBTIQ people in custody. It must've taken the prisoners a while to receive it, but once they had, incarcerated trans women immediately started writing to me. They had a litany of concerns, listed in long handwritten letters. They felt very intimate, unlike the calls and emails from my other clients. The letters detailed the sexual harassment, misgendering, violence and sexual assaults they experienced while in men's prisons around Victoria. They talked about the near impossibility of accessing gender-affirming healthcare and hormones while in custody, and the discrimination they'd faced in court from prosecutors, judges and even their own defence teams. I felt overwhelmed by this new cohort. I had been dimly aware of the plight of trans prisoners through Laverne Cox's portrayal of Sophia Burset on *Orange Is the New Black*. But unlike fictional Sophia, none of these trans women were housed in a women's prison. Even the trans women who had been on hormones prior to their incarceration got sent to men's prisons. Why was no one talking about this? I did what I could to help by writing letters to Corrections Victoria, alerting trans health services to their neglect and lodging detailed complaints with human rights commissions.

In a further effort to get my own life under control, I'd made a new year's resolution to amend my name and gender on the rest of my ID. I'd spent the few days before St Kilda Legal Service reopened contacting the Law Institute, my bank, utility companies and my phone and internet provider. There was no uniformity as to what documents each organisation required to make the changes. Some wanted a statutory declaration, while others wanted a letter from a doctor to confirm that I was 'receiving treatment for being transgender'. Some weren't really sure what their policy was and had just said to 'put it in writing', and then they'd work out what to do. I'd also gone through my inbox, unsubscribing to a slew of businesses that kept sending spammy emails to my old name. Whenever I thought I'd finally vanquished my administrative demons, another one would pop up. A toll fine for using the Eastlink without money in my online account reminded me I needed to update with them too, as well as VicRoads and my car insurer.

But I'd decided that the first order of business was my passport. I'd bundled that up with my change of name certificate, birth certificate and citizenship certificate, and then made an appointment with an Australia Post outlet near my work. I was buoyed by the fact that the chemist next door was cheerfully advertising the availability of Pre-exposure prophylaxis (PrEP) medication, which many gay and bi men took to lower their chance of HIV infection.

I waited in line on the grey-and-red carpet. The post office clerk greeted me warmly as I approached him at the counter.

'What can I help you with?' he asked.

'I need a new passport,' I said, pushing the application form towards him.

As he scrutinised it, his demeanour became chillier.

149

'Stay here,' he said, before going to the back room.

I stood at the counter, feeling awkward, while other customers filed in to complete their less problematic postal business. He was gone so long that the other staff member, a middle-aged woman, came over, smiled and asked what I needed help with. I showed her my paperwork and she too frowned then joined her colleague out back for a few moments. When he eventually returned, he failed to look at me at all, keeping his eyes on my paperwork and his computer. I saw him looking over my birth certificate. I was starting to feel quite defensive.

'So will you be taking my passport photos soon?' I asked.

'I'll take them when I am good and ready!' he snapped.

The line of customers all turned to watch us at this point, and I regretted choosing a post office so close to my work.

I feared him now, and I reverted into my shell to de-escalate the situation. I took out my phone, got onto the post office website and scrolled down to 'Make A Complaint'. A silent act of defiance. He eventually looked up from his screen and told me gruffly to move to the right so that he could take my passport photograph. He told me to take off my glasses. He didn't need to tell me not to smile.

I was officially having a shit day. I went back to the office and put my headphones on to listen to rain sounds to drown out my colleagues. I felt like I was failing Sandie by not being more supportive, but I had my own issues to deal with.

I hastily wrote an angry email, sent off my complaint and got an automatic reply, thanking me for my feedback and letting me know that I might be able to find an answer to my issue on their Help & Support page. I didn't take them up on that offer. On the upside, at least I now had a new scenario to add to my hypothetical ones showing how life would get worse for people like me if the Religious Discrimination Bill was passed. I poured my heart into describing a scene in which I'd actually been refused by the post office clerk and wasn't able to get a passport at all. What if I'd been in a hurry to reach a dying relative's hospital bed overseas? Or to offer a distant relative an organ donation? The consequences could be life or death. I crafted my story to create the most extreme unhappy ending. I couldn't tell if this was cathartic or making me more distressed.

I tried to reduce what had happened in the post office to a short explanation, like a case study I'd write for my clients. But what had actually happened? I'd got what I wanted; he didn't refuse me. I just felt crappy and sad. Microaggressions and low-level harm couldn't be easily captured in a case study. I had also, after all, voluntarily put myself in this new category of minority. Should I not be prepared to tolerate at least some pushback from people I interacted with who do not approve of my choices?

But my never-ending ID issues led me to a brain wave. Wouldn't it be amazing if there was one day a year that you could change all your ID at once with every organisation? I imagined a sea of stalls full of staff from Medicare, Centrelink, the passport office, banks and VicRoads, all trained in inclusive practice and ready to help. High on my dream, I contacted Transgender Victoria to see if they wanted to work together to make it happen. Beanie, the law student who'd booked me onto their student law panel the year before, emailed me back: *Sam, I'm the new events volunteer for Transgender Victoria. I'd LOVE to work with you on this.*

Over the next few weeks, we secured a venue at a huge warehouse-style community arts space in North Melbourne. I successfully applied for a quick response grant to pay for the space, the catering and fit-out, and for a graphic designer to make a cool poster. Beanie and I then arranged to meet up to nut out the finer details.

When Beanie came to visit me at Pink Panther, they were dressed in a campy, vintage, crushed velvet suit on top, with a pink ra-ra skirt, striped leggings and ballet flats on the bottom. They wore dark lipstick and eye shadow and had painted colourful faux freckles all over their face. Their unusual look was further accentuated by the large wicker basket they'd brought with them, filled with homemade baked cookies, wrapped in a red-and-white gingham tea towel. All in all, Beanie looked like a kaleidoscope of characters from a gothic story.

'They are vegan, gluten-free and low sugar,' Beanie told me as I bit into one of their cookies.

Given all that, it wasn't bad. I was hoping to sit down with Beanie for some serious event organising, but they insisted on going from desk to desk first to introduce themselves to the twenty Pink Panther staffers who were around and offering each of them a cookie. I wondered how long it might be until someone told me off for letting my guest roam around the office unchaperoned. I got started on writing a list of stakeholders to invite and was thoroughly absorbed in my task until Beanie gently put a hand on my shoulder, startling me.

'I tried to say hi to the CEO, but I was told by one of his assistants that he had to go into a big meeting,' they said.

I nodded, imagining what Neil must've thought of Beanie's moxie. *Well, fuck him,* I thought. Surely it was good for the head of an LGBTIQ health organisation to actually deal with a member of the community now and then?

We worked out the logistics of the event. I would organise the venue and manage the organisational invites, while Beanie would decorate the space and host the event. I was happier in the background, so this suited me well. I was a bit worried about safety, however. A few years back, some friends and I ran a regular queer night on Sydney Road in Brunswick called Orlando. One night, as a queer woman was leaving our event, she was dragged by the hair into a park by a group of men and sexually assaulted. A gay guy had been punched in the face and robbed as he took money out at a nearby ATM. As a group, we tried to figure out what to do. We didn't really want to hire security guards or to get the police involved, so we handed out flyers giving people information about what had happened, and advice about leaving in groups at the end of the night.

When Beanie finally floated off for the day, I slumped back into my chair. I couldn't imagine having all that energy. I was impressed by Beanie's commitment to courageously living a visibly gender-nonconforming life. Increasingly, that was just about the last thing I wanted to do. It felt like Beanie and I came from different eras, with far more than twelve years separating us.

* * *

As I continued to plan the accessibility measures for the event, I read more and more online about how trans and gender-diverse people are up to six times more likely than cis people to be diagnosed with autism. There were lots of guides about how to make events more accessible. They suggested that we turn off bright, direct or flashing lights, and try to establish a 'fragrance-free' environment without heavy perfumes or other artificial smells. Finally, they recommended a quiet space in which people who are overwhelmed can go to unwind and relax with beanbags, stim toys and water. This all sounded fantastic to me. So fantastic, in fact, that I began to wonder if I myself might be autistic.

I read more about the characteristics and how they present differently in people assigned female at birth, who often struggle to filter out background noise, are easily startled by loud noises, have trouble making eye contact and prefer one-on-one meet-ups to crowds. Masking, including mimicking the behaviour of those nearby, such as copying non-verbal behaviours, and developing complex social scripts to get by in social situations sounded deeply familiar to me. I began re-examining my life through the lens of autism. It was not difficult for me to find evidence of this theory. But I felt I had enough on my plate without taking on a new label.

When it came time to publicly announce the first ever Change Your ID Day, I posted about it all over social media:

> Join us at the Meat Market for Change Your ID Day, a one-stop shop for trans and gender-diverse people to change their name and gender on their driver's licence, passport, Medicare card and birth certificate. There will be a free vegan afternoon tea from the Asylum Seeker Resource Centre and live music by DJ Bangerz N Mash.

The event post was getting a lot of positive traction and was reshared by excited community members all over the internet. Within a day, the 150 free tickets we'd made available were all gone. Change Your ID Day was a sell-out.

I emailed Beanie to let them know the good news. I didn't hear back until the next day, when I read with increasing horror a long email they'd sent me at 3.30 a.m.

'I can't believe your rudeness and lack of foresight in publicly posting about this event before you'd cleared it with me. This has completely undermined the spoken word event I was planning to announce for International Day of Homophobia, Biphobia, Intersexism and Transphobia, which will occur BEFORE CHANGE YOUR ID DAY. Now no one wants to know about the first ever trans poetry slam that I've been coordinating. Everyone just wants to know about CHANGE YOUR ID DAY. As a result, I have reluctantly decided to cancel the poetry slam. I am very disappointed in you and have lost faith in our ability to collaborate on this project.'

I felt like I'd been punched in the gut. I thought we'd agreed on the advertising schedule, but maybe we hadn't. I looked back through my emails and there it was, an email I'd sent to Beanie suggesting that we kick off advertising four weeks before the event. But I resisted the temptation to send this evidence to them. I'd noticed that Beanie had a habit of swinging between an obsessive attention to detail to a complete disregard for the minor issues of dates and times. Perhaps I'd sent the email during one of Beanie's big-picture phases. No doubt

I could have reminded them before sending out the posts. I did tend to shoot from the hip, because I was so busy juggling my other work responsibilities.

I replied to Beanie with what I hoped was a sufficient apology. I ended the email by suggesting that Beanie end the event with some of their spoken word poetry to make up for the event they'd cancelled. A couple of days later, I received a blank email with an updated run sheet. Beanie had allocated themselves fifteen minutes for their 'final remarks'. I wasn't brave enough to ask for more details.

By the time the big day came around, I'd roped in a lot of volunteers, including Gemma, to help people check in, bump in and out, and manage any queues and bottlenecks.

I realised we didn't have a printer at the event, so I rushed down to JB Hi-Fi to buy one. There wasn't budget for this, but I figured it would be good to have one at home.

Since we'd never done any events like this before, we didn't quite know what to expect. I did expect the venue to be decorated, though. Beanie had sent me Pinterest vision boards and invoices for mounts of fabric, pride flags and throw rugs. Without all that, the concrete floors and original white brick walls gave a bit of a prison vibe, which was not what we were going for.

I tried calling Beanie. It rang out. I left a voicemail, even though I knew no one under thirty-five listened to them. I was then busy supervising the volunteers to set up tables and chairs before the representatives from the banks, government and local universities came in. Gemma was an angel, taking on the job of managing them all and getting them installed at their tables. Five minutes before we were due to open, Beanie still hadn't arrived, so I made some hasty notes on my phone of all the people I'd need to remember to thank when it came time for speeches. I tried calling Beanie one more time. Seconds later, I received a text back:

'Car trouble! Be there soon.'

When eleven a.m. rolled around – the advertised opening time – I started letting people in. Again, I was amazed to see so many trans and gender-diverse people together in the same room. This was a younger crowd, with plenty of ordinary, suburban-looking parents and caregivers by their sides. I suddenly felt overwhelmed by all the parental support. I couldn't imagine what having a life like that would feel like. I watched as more and more people filed in, meeting with enthusiastic departmental representatives, ready to do what they could to help people change their documents without fuss.

I was a bit starstruck when Precise walked in, an iconic figure around Collingwood. Often seen on a vintage lady's bicycle decorated with rainbow streamers and a bubble machine, Precise was the epitome of gender fluidity, with their skirt and pants combo, long pink hair and strong, masculine frame. They were a walking gender question marker. I really admired Precise's grit and determination to fly the flag of gender subversion at every intersection across Melbourne, despite that not being a life I wanted for myself. In my navy sweater and chinos, I felt like the most boring person in the room.

At 11.45 a.m., Beanie strode in wearing a full gold-and-burgundy medieval knight's costume, with billowing puffy velvet pants and clashing rainbow leggings. Atop their head sat a wine-red beret with a feather painted in blue, pink and white.

'I'm here!' Beanie declared, before swanning off to introduce them-selves to all the stallholders.

I was relieved to see them, as I'd convinced myself they were going to spend the day defaming me online instead of coming along to the event. Now that Beanie was here to take over as the master of ceremonies, I could relax. I wandered over to the low-sensory chill-out space, which we'd created to ensure the event was inclusive of neurodiverse people. I sat in a beanbag and quietly kneaded a squishy black kitten stress ball beside a couple of teens with their headphones on, before I was pulled away to answer one of the volunteers' questions.

As I walked back into the main room, I was overawed. The event was a total success. It didn't matter that there were no decorations. All the people streaming in throughout the day to get and receive help was a thing to behold. I was proud.

When it was time for speeches, Beanie rose to the occasion and did an excellent job of chairing. Although Beanie did slip in an impromptu rendition of a show tune from Kinky Boots halfway through, and ended the show with their own long, vitriolic poem about the pleasures of self-harm, we only finished five minutes over time. An amazing result for a queer event. As we were packing up, I felt – for the first time in a while – that it was cool to create events like this for a living.

Chapter 13
Chop Shop

It was getting cold again by the time my top surgery date finally arrived. Amongst all the other things on my mind, I'd forgotten Dr Desmond's warning to make sure my WPATH letter was dated less than three months before the surgery date. But when I emailed Dave, I got an out-of-office auto reply. He wasn't working there anymore. In fact, the Mind Equality Centre had disappeared altogether. The marriage equality guilt money must have dried up. I freaked out. How on earth was I going to get another letter in time? After many phone calls and much angst, someone from the Mind Australia head office took pity on me and got in touch with Dave. He then called me to check to see if anything had changed and then updated the letter for me. I felt like Dave was really going the extra mile for me, and I felt bad about all the mean things I'd said about him in my head.

I packed an overnight bag for what I'd jokingly called the most expensive hotel room in St Kilda. Over breakfast, Gemma gave me a beautiful yellow woollen blanket to mark the occasion. I held onto the blanket during the car ride over. As we walked into the glossy private hospital, I suddenly felt underdressed in the loose-fitting clothing I'd been advised to wear. Wealthy, glamorous women streamed in and out of the building, fresh from their cosmetic surgery appointments. We went up in the elevator to Dr Desmond's floor and were greeted by a receptionist. As we sat waiting to be admitted, I fumbled with my Medicare card, a back-up copy of my WPATH letter from Dave, and receipts for an $8000 payment to the hospital and a $2000 payment to the anaesthetist. I also brought along evidence of my top-level private insurance, which I had been advised to obtain the surgery was classed as an overnight psychiatric stay.

The receptionist called me up and carefully checked all my paperwork, and then a nurse showed us to a small room with a single bed and an ensuite, which I would be staying in overnight. Gemma helped me into a blue gown, booties and a hair net, and placed my new yellow blanket on the bed. As we sat around, I read up on the history of trans surgery law. I learnt that in 2004, Monash Gender Dysphoria Clinic and four of its specialists were sued by a former patient. The patient had been diagnosed with what was then known as 'transsexualism' in 1986 and had gender-affirming surgery in 1988. The person publicly celebrated their transition in a 1989 *Woman's Day* article. In 1996, they decided that this hadn't been the right thing for them after all, and detransitioned. The clinic, doctors and plaintiff eventually settled the case for an unstated sum of money. Given this history, I could now see why Dr Desmond had been so pedantic about the paperwork.

Gemma and I then kissed and said goodbye, and she left with tears in her eyes. A nurse came in to check my heart rate and blood pressure, and placed a plastic band around my wrist with my name and date of birth on it.

As he entered the room, Dr Desmond said, 'Hi, boss. Ready to go?' He asked me to strip down to my waist and then started sketching the now familiar arcs across my chest with a felt-tip pen. To try to reassure myself, I thought about the many hundreds of trans masculine people who'd had their surgeries before me in this very same hospital. It was pretty much a transgender production line here at this point.

I followed him into the operating theatre and lay down on the table. The nurses put surgical stockings on my legs and then a blanket over the bottom half of my body. The anaesthetist came in and introduced herself, then asked if I gave consent for her to go ahead. I nodded, and felt a light prick as the general anaesthetic was administered. As I began to enter the void, I worried that I might never wake up. I hoped that my legacy would not be the first trans person to die during top surgery.

Then everything went black.

* * *

When I woke up, I had already been wheeled back to my single room. Gemma was sitting next to me.

'How are you feeling?' she asked.

I tried to smile and say something, but I couldn't get any words out. 'Freezing,' I eventually said.

Gemma got up and added the yellow woollen blanket to my layer of blankets. My vision was blurry.

'How are you?' I said quietly, but I did not hear her answer as I fell back asleep.

* * *

An hour later, I woke up again as my friend Fabian came to visit. We played hangman on a whiteboard while I drifted in and out of sleep.

The next morning, I woke up when Gemma came back into my room. I was able to focus my eyes on the big white clock now. The time was 8.30 a.m.

'You look so much better today,' she said. 'Yesterday you looked grey. When they wheeled you in, I was terrified that you were dead.'

When I'd got out of theatre, she'd taken photos to show me later how dead I looked. I'd resembled a ghoul, with ashen skin and vacant eyes.

Gemma had brought a copy of *The Age* and we sat doing the quiz and the crossword, until the surgeon finally arrived to assess whether he could give me the all-clear to go home. He was satisfied when I confirmed that I'd been able to get up to go to the toilet and could carry out a conversation. I was the very image of a docile, grateful patient, and I thanked Dr Desmond profusely before he left.

A nurse with long, painted fingernails came in to pull out my canula. She got distracted halfway through, though, and a streak of bright red blood went all over the sheets and into the remote control for the TV. 'Oops,' she said, laughing. Gemma and I looked at each other in horror. It was a reminder of the deep cuts the surgeon had made during the procedure. Once she'd got the canula out correctly, I was allowed to put my trackpants and windcheater back on, and shuffled out the door in my tight black zip-up compression binder. I left with a packet of twenty Endone pills, a week's worth of antibiotics, and the strong recommendation that I pair each dose with a tall glass of Metamucil. Gemma bundled me up in the woollen blanket and drove me home. I watched the Orthodox private schools, organic greengrocers and Edwardian cottages go by until I fell asleep, waking up half an hour later back home in the west.

* * *

I spent my first day post-surgery napping on the couch. The next morning, when it was time for me to take off my bandages, I was nervous. I was squeamish about blood and unexpectedly frightened to see what my new, remodelled chest looked like. I slowly removed the dressings, and saw my own skin, without my breasts. My chest was puffy and bruised, and I had long pink scars on either side of my nipples. I showered gingerly, trying my best to take care of my wounded body. I felt like a construction site. *Am I insane?* I wondered. *Is this what insanity actually looks like, and everyone around me has been indulging me all this time?*

As I got out of the shower, Gemma knocked to come into the bathroom to see my new chest. She said that the surgeon had done an amazing job, and that I looked fantastic. I thought she was probably lying, but it was nice of her to say so. I put my tight black compression binder back on and zipped it up, and gingerly wrapped my bath towel around my waist instead of my chest. Another new gender convention to get used to.

I lay down again on the couch and tried to get up to date with the news. Beanie still hadn't called me out online, which was a relief. In a haze, I read about Tongan Australian Israel Folau's rugby union contract being terminated for saying on social media that homosexuals would be condemned to hell unless they repented for their sins. This sent the religious freedom debate into overdrive, and I was annoyed that I was now going to have to get my head around a whole other football code in order to follow the discussion. Despite the negative impact that his views would undoubtedly have on the Pasifika LGBTIQ community and any closeted athletes who might've looked up to him, I wasn't inclined to agree with the sacking of Israel Folau. For me, it was all too reminiscent of what happened to Roz Ward, the co-founder of the Safe Schools LGBTIQ education program, whose employment was terminated by La Trobe University in 2016 after she described the Australian flag as 'racist' on her private Facebook page. I just didn't think people should be sacked over their private social media usage. Like Ward and Folau, I too had a job that straddled the border between personal and professional identities. Of course, unlike myself or Ward, Folau was a powerful multi-millionaire, and I was all for sports brands tearing up their lucrative personal advertising contracts with him. But opposing his right to work seemed a step too far. The decision likely had more to do with protecting the inclusive image of Qantas and ASICS, Rugby Australia's major corporate sponsors, than the actual queer community. I felt more convinced of this after reading an open letter from a group of LGBTIQ elders from Tonga and Samoa, who had not called for Folau to be sacked but instead asked him to fund a Tongan LGBTIQ youth shelter that had just been ravaged by a cyclone.

Throughout the public debate about Folau, Rainbow Rights had been sending a flurry of emails asking for donations to support their campaign efforts. They had cluttered up my inbox even though I was sure I'd unsubscribed several times already. I looked up the *Spam Act* to see if I could report them. It all seemed a bit too hard, and almost certainly a dick move.

In the days after the surgery, I had drains sticking out of my chest that I carried around with me in a bright yellow tote bag, making me look like I was on a perennial mission to buy coffee and the newspaper. I had to milk the increasingly light pink fluid into the main chamber of the drains at night, as well as make a note on a chart of how much fluid I'd created in a day to tell nurse Mandy at my post-surgery check-up. Mandy was happy with my progress, and even beckoned me in with a flap of her fingers for a bearhug at the end of my appointment.

I received a care package from a group of community lawyers who'd attended the inclusive practice training I'd run. Looking through the basket full of cute socks, chocolates and some drawing supplies, I was very touched. I sat on the couch, drawing my hands drawing them-selves into existence, like the Escher lithograph.

* * *

I was still on leave from work on the day I was scheduled to give evi-dence at the Royal Commission into Victoria's Mental Health System. Dr Desmond had only just taken out my chest drains and I still had dressings over my scars, which I needed to change daily. On my way into the hearing, I was called 'sir' by one of the security guards and then 'ma'am' by the next. Despite the surgery, I was still evidently in the he/she era.

I sat in the waiting room for an hour, where Debbie found me and asked me if I wanted some tissues. I told her that I was okay, and then she asked if I wanted some food. I wasn't really hungry, but I felt like

I should give Debbie the opportunity to perform her official role of helper. 'That would be lovely, thanks,' I said.

She came back five minutes later with some Greek salad and rice noodles on a paper plate, with a single disposable wooden knife. 'I had to sneak into the commissioner's area to get this for you. I'm so sorry, I couldn't find a fork.'

I smiled, took the food, and ate my artfully crafted morsels by hand.

After a couple of hours watching the live stream of the hearings from the waiting room, I was collected by Debbie as my name would be called next. When I heard my bland pseudonymous name, I stood up and walked into the witness box. As I passed the audience, I felt everyone staring at me, likely wondering what such a boring little man could possibly have to say. The lead commissioner explained to the audience that I had asked for the live feed to be cut and that my identity was the subject of a suppression order, which I'd asked for to protect my professional reputation. It would be a criminal offence for anyone in the public gallery to record or broadcast my statement.

And then we were on. Claudia, who was in a full wig and gown, asked me to affirm the truth of my written statement and to promise to tell the truth, which I did. I wasn't sure if I was meant to look at Claudia or the commissioners, so I switched between them. The male commissioner on the right looked particularly uninterested, like he might nod off to sleep at any moment after a long, boozy day at the races.

As it turned out, giving evidence was far easier than leading evidence from my clients. I even began to enjoy myself at times, finding that I had all the answers to Claudia's very leading questions, since all I was required to do was recount my own experiences. The only real disadvantage of being in the witness box was that, unlike all of the other lawyers present, I wasn't being paid to be there.

After the hearing was over, I saw Tobi, a gender nonconforming former colleague, who had watched me give evidence.

'Sorry, Sam, when I saw you I assumed you were giving evidence on behalf of your work, not about your own experiences. I wouldn't have sat in if I'd known,' said Tobi.

'Never mind,' I replied.

And just then, I really didn't mind. I was almost relieved to be seen closer to who I truly was: a sad, troubled individual who was doing their best to find care, rather than a professional who didn't have personal difficulties and whose job was to solve everyone else's.

But this relief soon turned into toxic shame at having revealed too much of myself, of having been a show-off, a fraud, a fool. The feelings were enough to overwhelm my pride at having been brave enough to share my story, and to have lived through my difficult experiences. Instead, I was consumed by the thought that I'd been complicit in legitimising a process I didn't entirely agree with – or, worse, that I was an Uncle Tom type in the proceedings, providing a largely cisgender audience with an eloquent, relatable figure instead of someone who was so angry they couldn't speak because of all the indignities they'd suffered.

I fumed at myself for agreeing to participate in this public showcase when I was still wrapped in bandages and a post-surgical chest binder, deeply afraid of looking at the wounds that lay beneath. It seemed to me then that my giving evidence was not an example of my resilience, but a manifestation of my own shame and self-loathing, which meant I would say yes to almost any task presented to me, no matter the personal cost.

* * *

The first time I put a t-shirt on without my compression binder felt momentous. I walked down Barkly Street in Footscray with Gemma, same as any other day. But under the surface, I felt – for a brief second – a moment of pure joy. It was a relief to run my fingers along my now reasonably flat chest, occasionally forgetting that it was currently held together with a few dissolving stitches and scar-reducing surgical tape. I'd kept my nipples, which were reshaped into little raspberry-looking things and moved to a brand-new location. Although I wasn't in a lot of pain, I couldn't lift my arms. I was afraid of opening my wounds and having to return to a hospital, so I was very careful.

I donated my compression binder, along with all my other binders, to Transgender Victoria. I gave some of my sports bras to Gemma and donated dozens of the child-sized singlets I'd worn over the years to a local op-shop. It took weeks to walk without being highly attuned to my flayed upper body and days before I slept comfortably. Over the next few months, I had intermittent zapping sensations as my nerve endings recovered from the surgery. I felt amazed by my own body and its ability to heal from the trauma.

Chapter 14
TERF Wars

By the time I'd made it to South Melbourne's imposing town hall, I was late. The Acknowledgement of Country was underway, so I quickly took a seat on one of the few empty chairs, beside an older lesbian duo around a circular table. I glanced enviously at them as they poured piping hot tea from a well-worn tartan thermos, sensibly dressed in fleecy Kathmandu jackets to match the biting day outside. One wore rounded, black-rimmed glasses that were exactly like mine. In fact, she looked the way I supposed I would've at sixty if I hadn't transitioned.

I watched as the Boon Wurrung Elder handed the mic to the LGBTIQ Commissioner, who thanked them and began a pre-prepared speech.

'The Victorian Pride Centre will be a state-of-the-art, 6000-square-metre building, bringing various organisations together to deliver a holistic, multifaceted approach to celebrating and empowering LGBTIQ communities and individuals.'

A small architectural model of the unique circular white building was wheeled out by a volunteer, to many oohs and aahs. It looked like a fancy wedding cake that a huge drill had just ploughed through.

I'd heard on the grapevine that any future state government funding for the Queer Legal Service would be tied to it being located at the Pride Centre, so I felt I had to take an interest. Almost everyone I knew thought it was a terrible location, since St Kilda wasn't particularly easy to get to by car or public transport. But the Victorian government had sunk a lot of money and political capital into the project and wanted it to be successful. Pink Panther was meant to be taking the entire top floor of the new building, so as long as we kept getting funding to maintain our partnership, I'd presumably move over with its team when the time came.

As the Commissioner's speech droned on, I kept looking up at the big white clock, already desperate for a morning tea break. When the commissioner finished, the woman in glasses beside me quickly raised her hand.

'This sounds like yet another one of these "umbrella places" that doesn't meet the needs of older lesbians,' she said. 'If we book one of these rooms, what assurances can you give us that we'll be allowed to confine our meetings to women-born women?' The woman beside her furiously nodded.

Murmurs of discontent broke out across the room, and more hands went up. The commissioner quickly returned to the mic. 'The Pride Centre will be for the whole community to access. You can, of course, host member-only meetings for AGMs and planning days, but it will be a space where respect and non-discrimination will be expected from all users,' they replied.

'Nobody wants to come to your TERFy meetings anyway!' a woman in a frilly pink top yelled to scattered laughter.

My neighbour's hand shot back up. 'If that's the kind of respect that we can expect at your new "Pride Centre", then I am sure we're not interested,' she said, and the two women got to their feet.

'I urge you to stay and continue the discussions throughout the day,' said the commissioner. It seemed half-hearted.

'Since your department has repeatedly rejected every funding application we've made,' the woman in the glasses said, 'and refused to take on board any of our recommendations, I don't think we'll waste any more of our time. It's clear none of you are interested in meeting the needs of lesbians.'

They collected their things as the room looked on, lips curled into half smiles. Their footsteps in their matching brown Blundstones echoed throughout the room as they departed. I was left alone at the table.

'Coffee break?' asked the Commissioner.

Chairs scraped along the hardwood floors as people made a beeline for the big silver urns at the back of the room. I decided I needed something stronger and headed outside, towards the nearest espresso bar. As my eyes adjusted to the sunlight, I noticed the lesbians backing out of a parking spot in a forest-green Subaru Outback. My dream car. So sturdy and practical for camping.

As I waited for my coffee, Morgen walked in, a trans woman I knew from my old call centre days who'd also been at the meeting. Her hair was freshly dyed in shades of purple, teal and red.

'What just happened?' I asked.

'Oh, them. They're the OLGAs, the Older Lesbians Guild of Australia. All two of them. They've got a bee in their bonnet about us identifying as lesbians and then forcing them to have sex with us. I mean, as if, right?' she said, with a dramatic flick of her hair.

'God, I had no idea. I thought that breed of lesbian feminism was confined to the UK,' I replied.

'Honey, if you're going to be trans in this town, you're going to learn all about our homegrown TERFs.'

She wasn't wrong.

* * *

A month later, Morgen invited me to attend a university forum on transgender rights. I'd vaguely followed the brouhaha that a few radical feminist philosophy academics had been making about the proposed birth certificate law reform in Victoria. Trans groups had been campaigning to change the law to allow people to amend the gender marker on their birth certificates without first undergoing genital surgery.

One of the academics had organised a forum titled 'The Threat to Sex-Based Rights' at their campus to express their opposition to the self-ID laws. In response, the campus queer collective asked the university to cancel the event because it could cause psychological and emotional harm to trans students and staff. The vice-chancellor refused, on the grounds of academic freedom. Campus security prevented protesters from entering the building, and attendees were subject to ID and bag checks.

In the days following the event, stickers appeared in toilets across the university likening trans women to convicted rapists, causing further outrage. Things had got ugly.

When I arrived on campus that evening, I immediately noticed the wall of large pink, blue and white posters adorning every bollard leading to the lecture theatre. Their main text read, 'No Transphobia in Our Tutes'. I peered at the smaller writing. Apparently, some of the set texts in the undergraduate Feminism course denigrated transgender people, and the student union was calling on its members to boycott the subject.

The lecture theatre was full to the brim with students and staff. Flags for transgender, non-binary and asexual rights decorated the front of the room, creating a cacophony of colour to rival the original pride flag itself.

I took a seat at the back as Rupert, a short trans man with a goatee, wireframed glasses and a blue suede jacket, opened the meeting. Beside him were several trans women I recognised, including Morgen – in a shimmering rainbow dress covered with sequins – world-renowned sociology academic Professor Emerita Raewyn Connell and Amao Leota Lu, a Samoan fa'afafine performance artist, poet and community activist.

'Hi, everyone, it's great to start this much-needed conversation on trans politics in university life and beyond. Each panellist will give a five-minute speech, followed by a Q and A session where you can ask questions via an app which will appear on the screen above,' said Rupert.

Professor Connell began. 'We need to situate this debate in twentieth-century feminist history. During the 1970s many women made powerful efforts to set up women's refuges, community health centres and community legal services to address the inequities built into our system. Some other feminists, however, derided these step-by-step efforts, and sought to create a separate women's-only society. As they concentrated on this task, they increasingly focused on purifying the movement of the small number of transgender women in these circles. The work of Sheila Jeffreys typified this approach. I nonetheless believe that feminism is the most vital ideology for trans people to understand how to advance our own equality.'

Next, Morgen – who'd added a red feather boa to her outfit – strode up to the microphone. 'We need to change things so that trans people can enrol in university or apply for a job without having to out ourselves by presenting a birth certificate that doesn't match our outward appearance. Requiring people to get lower surgery to be recognised as who they are is tantamount to forced sterilisation, not to mention that hardly anyone can afford these procedures. It's got to stop,' Morgen said, to rapturous applause.

Amao Leota Lu then addressed the imposition of Western European gender norms on Pasifika peoples, and its impact on trans women of

173

colour. 'These harmful debates in the academy trickle down to the murder of brown trans girls on the streets,' she said, stunning the room into silence.

Every speaker had so much to say that they went way over their allocated five minutes, so the meeting was already running late by the time we got to the Q&A. I was ravenous and considered making a hasty exit, until I saw the audience questions come up on the big screen. In amongst supportive messages were some unexpectedly biting questions:

> 'Why do the men (so-called "trans women") feel that they can speak on behalf of ordinary women?'
> – Anonymous User_01

> 'Why does the $*&% in the feather boa feel the need to parody women-born women by dressing in a grotesque hyper-feminine way?'
> – Anonymous User_03

> 'Are you just a bunch of autogynephilic fetishists backed by big pharma $$$$ brainwashing children to mutilate themselves to justify your "identities"?'
> – Anonymous User_06

I watched on in horrified fascination. The TERFs had obviously infiltrated the event, and all was not going to plan. I looked around the room to see who might be responsible for the anonymous questions. Were they sitting next to me again? I peered at the people to my left and right. Everyone had their heads buried in their phones. It was hard to tell what anyone thought. I watched these questions get upvoted and downvoted in turn, as other questions flooded the screen in support of transgender rights.

Rupert looked spooked. Morgen picked up the mic. 'I have a right to speak as a woman because trans women are women!' she said, getting a standing ovation.

The mood was electric, and I was anxious that things would escalate if the audience members who'd posted the anonymous questions revealed themselves to the room. What if the crowd decided that I was one of them? I wished I'd bought one of the pink-and-blue lanyards that had been for sale at the entrance.

One of the event organisers quietly whispered into Rupert's ear, who then promptly wrapped up the meeting. Everyone looked emotionally exhausted and suspicious.

As the crowds walked towards the exits, I went down to the front of the lecture theatre to say goodbye to Morgen. Before giving me a kiss goodnight on the cheek, she said, 'Well, I think we can all agree the Q&A section was a tactical error on our part.'

When my head hit my pillow, my mind swirled with images of the thorny questions, which replayed in my mind throughout the night. I felt unsettled. Why were these women so angry about trans people? Were they genuinely worried about being sexually assaulted by trans women in toilets, or was that just a scare campaign? What was all this doing to our collective mental health?

* * *

I went back on antidepressants. I'd been on and off them for a decade. Every time I thought I could say goodbye to them forever, the familiar sound of the plastic packet popping open re-entered my life. It seemed I was hooked on big pharma forever.

In the months that followed, my face and body continued to morph, and I began to be perceived as male more of the time. At first it was a surprising novelty, but before long I began to feel a deep frustration whenever anyone referred to me as 'she'. I was crossing over but hadn't quite arrived at my destination. The constant uncertainty about how each person would read my gender made me moody and withdrawn. I longed to go into a cave to hibernate, only emerging when my appearance would no longer cause baristas confusion.

The campaign for birth certificate law reform continued. The newspapers were saying that the Births, Deaths and Marriages Registration Amendment Bill was likely to pass thanks to a sympathetic state Labor government with a big majority. But a similar bill was narrowly defeated in 2016, so everyone was nervous. Despite my desire for invisibility, I dragged myself down to a rally at State Library Victoria in support of my own kind. I listened to speeches by activists and parents of transgender children, while a Labor-backed rainbow rights lobby group handed out colourful placards that read, 'My Identity, My Choice' and 'Autonomy and Freedom'. I stood in a group holding them as we posed for photos with tight, painted-on smiles.

With every public event came more articles and opinion pieces in the media for or against, with members of OLGA and the self-described 'gender critical' feminist academics taking every opportunity to share their opposition with the public.

Everything I read made me more and more frustrated. Did they really think that this was the number-one issue facing women? What about domestic violence, family annihilators, the gender pay gap or rising rates of homelessness? Why did they have to pick on us when there were so many other things to worry about?

I got sucked into reading endless debates on Twitter with hashtags like #LGBwithouttheT, #BiologyIsNotBigotry and #AdultHumanWoman. Some of the comments were amusing: 'It's all well and good you are people pretending to be men, but you can't change what's on the inside. When you're a skeleton, archaeologists won't have any trouble picking you out as the females you are.'

Being misgendered by an archaeologist hundreds of years after my death was not high up on my list of concerns. What would last longer, the gender binary or the human race? Perhaps catastrophic climate change will resolve the gender wars for us. No cross-sex hormones on a dead planet.

One day, I walked past Sheila Jeffreys' newest book at the library. I didn't want to be the kind of person who wouldn't engage with the other side of a debate, so I decided to read it cover to cover. She was the same age as my mum. Like me, she was born in England and migrated to Melbourne as an adult. Her life of radical student meetings and niche debates in political reading groups filled me with nostalgia for my own university days. But despite our similarities, I found her core beliefs increasingly bizarre. She argued that the phenomenon of trans women was an extension of 'penile imperialism', in which men are assumed to have the right to access women's bodies and their spaces. She then claimed that 'transgenderism' is a condition created by a medical system that seeks to reinforce traditional gender roles and generate profit through required therapy, hormone replacement and surgery. This did not accord with my own experiences of accessing gender-related healthcare. In the short time I'd been on testosterone, the most popular gel had been permanently taken off the market, leading to shortages in all other brands and fear about what might go next. While the handful of surgeons who performed gender-affirming surgery in Australia were no doubt getting rich off the backs of trans people, it was a drop in the ocean compared with the money they were making from mainstream cosmetic surgeries.

As I read on, I began to think that I could've done a better job of lampooning the transgender rights movement myself. But Jeffreys said something that struck a nerve. She claimed that 'female-bodied transgenders' (i.e., people like me) were escaping misogyny by masquerading as men, and that we should instead be fighting for a world where women can have short hair, wear jeans and not act in typically 'feminine' ways without feeling the need to transition.

Was my decision to transition another blow to women's liberation, flattening the possibilities of what it means to be a woman? Should I have resisted my desire to present as male, instead showing the next generation of masculine girls that they can live as they are without taking male hormones?

As the debate about the birth certificate law reform continued to swirl around the internet, the online behaviour of some members of the trans community seemed to escalate along with it. First, there was the blow-up over a trans woman telling trans men that they all needed to shave their neckbeards. I thought it was funny, and immediately got my razor out to tidy myself up. But the post caused a giant Twitter fight that went on for weeks. Some said the comment was fucked because it replicated sexist power structures, and that people assigned female at birth should never be told what to do with their body hair. My mind was in knots, trying to carefully work my way through the logic of each clamorous debate.

In the online mess, I discovered a whole new sub-group, trans TERFs. They argued that while it was fine for them to access gender-af-firming care, this trans thing had really gone too far. They believed that the biggest threat to their access to hormone therapy was the dangerous efforts of trans rights activists to expose children to 'trans ideology', which would ultimately lead to a backlash. Some of them said that most trans women weren't actually transgender but instead were experiencing a condition called 'autogynephilia', where a male becomes sexually attracted to the idea of themselves as female. My head was officially spinning.

One morning I woke up to find my Twitter feed full of comments relating to a teenage trans girl live-tweeting her suicide attempt. She then went on to criticise Lifeline for breaching her confidentiality by calling emergency services to save her life. She said that she couldn't handle the hatred anymore. I decided to deactivate my account.

* * *

Morgen asked me to come to Parliament House with her to meet with a left-libertarian politician who wanted to hear the views of the trans community on the proposed reforms. When I arrived and began reading from a short, prepared speech, she smiled warmly and cut me off.

'Really, don't bother. Of course I'll vote for the new laws. I've just had so many meetings with TERFs about this bill over the last few weeks that I was desperate to see some friendly faces. God, who made those dykes the arbiters of womanhood? They are literally the worst-dressed women I've ever seen!' she said with a laugh.

I felt stung on their behalf. Despite their opposition to my existence, I still had a greater sense of kinship with them than this slim woman with long blonde hair in a fashionable silver dress. Her remarks reeked of lesbophobia. Couldn't she see that I'd looked like them until just a few months ago?

On the day of the vote, I went along to parliament to watch it with a group of trans advocates. I hadn't planned on going but I found myself drawn there, unable to tear myself away from history unfolding.

The radical feminist contingent had also arrived to bear witness to the 'death of their sex-based rights'. The parliamentary staff ensured that the two opposing groups were seated at each end of the public viewing station, separated by a red velvet rope. There were no transgender politicians in parliament to speak up for the bill, nor any radical feminists to oppose it. It was left to the religious conservatives to make the case for them. A bullish-looking MP called Bernie Finn began by calling the bill an 'attack on our society'.

'There are two genders. Of the two genders, there is the male – there is homosexual inclination and various paedophilic inclinations, there are a whole range of inclinations, and we could go on with that for quite some time. But in terms of gender, there are only two genders: male and female. I do not want a man who claims to be a woman to get a birth certificate which says that he is a woman. I do not want him to get that birth certificate and use that to molest women, to molest young girls, as some inevitably will.'

It was galling to sit quietly in that extravagant red room, listening to this man say these things for as long as he chose to. I wondered what the radical feminists on the other side of the rope thought of their champion.

The bill finally passed twenty-six to fourteen in the Victorian upper house that evening. Our side hugged and cheered in the parliamentary hallway. I didn't feel happy so much as relieved that we wouldn't have to talk about it anymore. The Commissioner appeared from a side room to shake Florence's hand. No doubt Rainbow Rights would be showering themselves in glory at a fancy bar soon. I guess they'd probably done a lot to make it happen, but I found the way they pushed themselves into the middle of every media narrative at the expense of all other organisations very obnoxious. I supposed it was a consequence of their need to constantly hustle for funding.

The radical feminists quietly filed out in their sensible jackets, faces drawn yet defiant. I saw the lesbian with the glasses from the Pride Centre walking along with them. Where did she drive her Subaru home to at night? Why did she have so much skin in this game? I didn't feel any malice towards her, just sadness that two peas in a pod like us could be so irretrievably divided. It reminded me of the meme of Spider-Man pointing at Spider-Man, near body doubles, locked forever in an endless battle.

Chapter 15
Detachable Penis

I'd been self-consciously avoiding mirrors for months, but finally decided to take a good look at myself. I'd had the same regulation millennial haircut for a decade – short back and sides with a sweeping side part. But at some point, my hairline had changed. Once resembling an upside-down U, it now appeared more like a right-side-up M. My nostrils were thinner, my cheeks flattened. I was still wearing the same beaten-up rounded tortoiseshell glasses frames I'd had for years. My eyes, previously large and quizzical, were now narrower, more inscrutable, as my brow and orbital bones became more pronounced.

My face was wider than before, with a redistribution of my facial fat deposits emphasising my jawbone. My pale skin, once soft and flawless, was now thicker, rougher and oilier, with larger pores and fuzzy facial hair. My neck could now sit comfortably on the body of a rugby player. All these changes were hard to put your finger on individually, but all came together to make me look male.

But if I was looking male, I was not feeling particularly male, whatever that meant. I felt like an imposter any time I went into male spaces. I made another big foray into the men's club by making a snap-second decision to drop into a barber's shop on Carlisle Street on my lunch break. Even though the sign on the door said, 'Walk-in's welcome', I was sure they were going to ask me to come back when I had an appointment.

The solo barber, a man in his thirties with a thick, well-oiled beard and hip vintage tattoos, was giving a man in a black barber's chair a shave with a straight-edge razor. The barber gestured for me to take a seat on an overstuffed red leather couch.

'Beer?' he asked me.

It was Tuesday at midday, and I was just across the road from my workplace. Polina could walk past at any moment.

'Sure, thanks,' I replied, and was soon sipping from a tall silver can of Asahi.

When he finished up with his other customer, the barber sat me down in his chair. I was nervous. Perhaps I could pass in the men's toilets, where patrons barely glanced at each other. But would my new-found masculinity hold up to thirty minutes of professional scrutiny?

'So, what are we doing today?' he asked, as he ran his fingers through my hair.

I realised I had no vocabulary for the next step. What had I even said when I got my hair cut at a women's hairdresser? They always just seemed to know what to do.

'Just the same, but, you know, shorter?' I replied.

'You want a tapered fade at the back?' he asked.

'Yep,' I replied.

'One to two?' he asked.

'For sure,' I said.

I had no idea what I had just agreed to. He began buzzing the back of my neck. I realised this was going to be much shorter than my usual haircut. I tried to relax into it. I closed my eyes and listened to the noises around me. Tupac was playing through a JBL Boombox in the corner of the room, and I could faintly hear road noises from the intersection of Carlisle and Chapel streets.

I took another sip of Asahi. *This is the life*, I thought. I looked around the shop. There were vinyl records and prints of Jimi Hendrix and Muhammad Ali on the walls, beside a sturdy oak cabinet which housed a display of men's pomades and waxes.

Male space. It was funny. This was a place where men groomed each other, so they had to butch it up to compensate.

When the barber finished up, my hair was shorter than it had ever been. I rubbed the back of my neck to feel the smooth, spiky remnants. I paid on my card, shocked to discover that I was only being charged $38. That was a quarter of the price I usually paid to get my hair cut.

As soon as I started passing, I never looked back. I stopped using they/them pronouns. No more of this 'busting the binary' business. I just wanted to move through the world with a minimum of fuss. And, unsurprisingly, living the life of a white man in Australia was incredibly easy. I started getting served at bars without waiting for fifteen minutes, and people stopped talking over me in meetings. Even people who had known me pre-transition seemed to treat me with more respect. But while things were going swimmingly as I started passing full-time as male, the incongruence of my genitalia became a more pressing concern for me. The testosterone had deepened my voice, widened my neck and gifted me a jungle of arse hair, but it could not, of course, provide me with a penis.

It had done something down there, however. I read that the technical term for my new 'condition' was clitoromegaly – in simple terms, an enlarged clitoris. In the definitive *Atlas of Human Sex Anatomy*, the typical clitoris is defined as being 3–4 millimetres in width and 4–5 millimetres in length. When I first started researching transitioning, I was alarmed about this side effect of testosterone usage.

I spent hours on trans forums reading about other trans people's experiences of this. I learnt that some call it their 'dick', their 'growth' or their 'junk'. Of those, I decided I liked 'junk' the best. Like a beat-up old jalopy, 'junk' is fun, cheap and cheerful, the kind of miscellany you might find in the discount bin of a country op shop. The trans men and non-binary folk on Reddit and Facebook are always talking about their 'junk'. Some crow about their 2–3-inch growth, while others ask what they can do to get to these great lengths. Solutions are offered, including clitoral pumps and ointments, though there's little proof that they work.

I read that depending on the shape of your vulva, you might feel discomfort when your nub starts rubbing up against your underwear. I didn't have this problem. My little nub was safely stored away behind the folds of my labia majora.

I was surprised to find that trans men engaged in as much size talk online as their cisgender counterparts. Because I don't think in inches, it took me a while to realise what they meant. Five to seven centimetres? Mine was nowhere near that. I realised then that, even by trans man standards, I was on the small side.

Passing created the new dilemma of where to piss. It was one thing using the men's toilets at Pink Panther, but quite another to go into the men's toilet at a packed bar or during rush hour at Flinders Street Station, where a free stall with a functional door could be hard to come by. Even when I found one, as I sat down to wee I'd be gripped by worry. What if a man entered the next stall, looked down and noticed that my feet weren't facing the wall? So, it wasn't just a question of where to urinate, but how.

I looked into stand-to-pee (STP) devices. There was a seemingly endless array of consumer choices, from top-end prosthetics – designed with care, right down to realistic skin folds – to the DIY folded yoghurt-pot lids that wikiHow showed me how to craft.

One time, when I was hanging around in the city while waiting to meet up with Gemma, I wandered into a camping shop to look for an STP. The one they sold was known as the Shewee. It had a sleek purple sheath attached to a thin, shallow, pointed funnel. Marketed as 'the original female urination device since 1999', the Shewee promised me the freedom to pee simply and hygienically without removing a single item of clothing. It was even NATO-approved for use by women in the military.

I went up to the counter with my Shewee, uncertain how this purchase would be interpreted. When the man at the counter said something unintelligible to me, I started sweating. Was he making fun of me?

'Sorry, what was that?' I asked.

'Are you a member of Lone Wolf Camping?' he sighed.

'Oh, no.'

'That'll be $22.95,' he said.

I tapped my card and stuffed my contraband into my backpack. I wanted to try it right away, but I needed to fill up my bladder first. I went into the first drinking den I saw, which turned out to be an old-fashioned whisky bar. With its polished wood countertops, framed images of male athletes and sturdy leather couches, I was beginning to detect a theme. I quickly finished off a pint of beer then shut myself in the sole stall in the men's toilets. As men came in and out to use the urinals, I stood facing the toilet, ready to use my Shewee. I cupped the purple plastic underneath my vulva, and tried my best to relax while conjuring a waterfall. I must've done this too well because my flow almost immediately burst the Shewee's dams, and urine streamed into my underpants and down my legs. I then had to dash into Myer to buy a new pair of jeans and some underwear before dinner.

When I got home, I forgot to wash it, and it remained at the bottom of my backpack for weeks. When I finally fished it out in horror, the

Shewee was covered in a spider web of thin green mould. The Shewee had to go.

During all of my private gender mishaps, my own sense of self was never far from my mind. What was I – a male with a vagina, or a mannish woman with a supersized clitoris and a hairy tummy? Maybe I'd crossed over into the land of the third sex, like Hermaphroditus, a male and female conjoined. Perhaps I'd become, through hormonal intervention, physically intersex. I kept searching back through time to find a sense of cultural lineage as I continued to try to understand myself.

After Edward De Lacy Evans, I next became fascinated by Harry Crawford. Also dubbed a 'male impersonator' by the media, he was sent to Sydney's Long Bay jail in 1920 for the murder of his wife. The prosecution argued that Crawford had killed her after she discovered that he was biologically female. Describing Crawford as 'practical in her deceit', the prosecution tantalised the press by indirectly alluding to the 'false phallus' confiscated during a raid on Crawford's home. The Crown never produced the unmentionable item, deemed too scandalous to be seen by the public. Despite little direct evidence or certainty that the burnt body that was found was even his wife's, Crawford was convicted, his capital sentence commuted to life. But what happened to the fake penis? How did he construct it? I wondered if it was still hiding in an evidence bag somewhere, just waiting to be displayed at the Justice and Police Museum. Could I book in to visit it, if I was ever game enough to ask?

I read even more historical accounts of people across Great Britain and the United States who had lived as I now did. There were books about James Barry, Alan L. Hart and Sir Ewan Forbes, who lived as men and worked as medical practitioners. I was particularly struck by the life of nineteenth-century hunter and memoirist Joseph Lobdell. Assigned female at birth in New York State, he lived as a male for sixty years before being arrested for vagrancy while subsisting in the forest with his wife and pet bear. Upon his admission to the Willard Insane Asylum in Ovid, New York, Lobdell said, 'I may be a woman in one sense, but I have peculiar organs that make me more a man than a woman.' A report from his psychiatrist goes on to say, 'She says she has the power to erect this organ in the same way a turtle protrudes its head – her own comparison.'

I felt a deep kinship with this strange wandering man, now lost to the grave.

* * *

After a little while back on the job post-surgery, I found that I was developing a chronic fear of answering the telephone, and I felt sick with worry every time I opened my inbox. My file notes were full of increasingly crazed doodles I'd draw while listening to my clients' sad stories on the phone.

When I'd get home from work, I felt gloomy and irritable, with a constant sense that I was failing my clients, Gemma, and the few friends I'd managed to keep in touch with.

With every day that passed, I looked less and less like the slightly awkward but oh-so eager-to-please soft butch pixie in my ID photo for my Pink Panther lanyard, and more like a small, morose man. The testosterone had aged me too; I began to look closer to my actual age of thirty-five than I ever had before. My Peter Pan days were officially over.

I also developed insomnia. I'd wake up at 3.30 a.m. most nights and be unable to get back to sleep for hours. I took all kinds of online personality tests, lost in the kind of self-obsession that hadn't beset me since my teens. I learnt that I was an INTJ in the Myers–Briggs scale, 'The Investigator' in the Enneagram's and that my work DiSC style was C/D.

I went onto the Death Clock, which calculated the likely date of your death based on your age, size, lifestyle habits and, importantly, sex.

I tried it as female first: 'You will live to be eighty-eight years, six months and one day old! Based on our calculations, you will die on: Thursday, 21 April 2072.' I then changed my answer to male: 'You will live to be eighty-three years, nine months and twenty days old! Based on our calculations, you will die on: Tuesday, 9 August 2067.' Would the testosterone really take five years off my life? If so, it seemed like a reasonable trade-off.

I then switched over to see what questions were being asked in my local Melbourne trans masc Facebook group. The same topics kept popping up over and over again, like 'which private insurer covers top surgery' and 'which GP can I see to get prescribed testosterone in Werribee/Shepparton/Frankston?' I then read a question which I hadn't seen come up before.

'Hey, I really want to get a phalloplasty. I know there's only one dude that does it in Australia and it's like pretty expensive. Are there any options people know of that are actually financially viable for someone on welfare?'

His question, which I could not answer, touched a nerve within me. Over the next few nights of intermittent sleep, I learnt all there was to know about phalloplasty. There was a whole new array of terminology to get my head around, which seemed to mainly relate to where the surgeon took the skin from, usually the forearm, leg or lower abdomen. The trauma to the donor site is significant, with huge scars that take years to fully heal. Once they've got the skin, the surgeon then shapes and contours this stolen flesh and attaches it to the groin. At this stage, the patient has something that resembles a penis, but it can't get up to too much.

The second stage, scheduled about six months later, includes lengthening the urethra to allow for urination out of the tip of the penis, creating the scrotum from genital tissue, and removing the vagina. All that original plumbing has got to go. Finally, a year later, they put in saline testicle implants and an inflatable erectile device to help the patient achieve an erection. Then, presumably, you rest.

My extensive midnight research revealed that lots can go wrong with phalloplasty. There are moments of pain and unexpected leakage. Bladder and rectal injuries, frequent urinary tract infections and incontinence. Multiple follow-up appointments and unforeseen hospitalisations. Functional limitations on the arm or leg from which the tissue was removed. Unsatisfactory penis length or testicle size.

I learnt that phalloplasty was not devised for the purposes of gender reassignment, but in response to the tidal wave of lower-body blast wounds experienced by male soldiers during World War I. The first phalloplasty for gender reassignment was performed in 1946 by the New Zealand physician Sir Harold Gillies on a fellow doctor, Laurence Michael Dillon (born Laura Maud Dillon). It involved thirteen procedures and remained the standard technique for forty years. I saw that Michael Dillon had moved to India, become a Buddhist and changed his name to Lobzang Jivaka after being outed by the press. I ordered his memoir online, and then fell back asleep.

Another evening, I was excited to see that I'd been accepted into a secret Facebook group called 'Jason's Phallo Journey', after my request had sat pending for a week. I leaned forward in bed, eager to know everything about Jason's new member. In his profile image, Jason beams in a fancy button-up shirt, arm in arm with a long-haired woman in a sensible blouse and pleated blue skirt, smiling lovingly at him. They might have been at a vineyard wedding. I scrolled to the start of Jason's journey, when he was about to go into surgery for his hysterectomy, lots of 'good luck' messages posted next to an image of him in a hospital gown. A week later, there's a photo of his hairy abdomen with fresh pinhole surgery scars. Six months later, he's back in a hospital bed for procedure number two. He sounded tired and sore afterwards; the Endone helped with the pain but made him constipated. Procedure three was tricky, and he was soon in a hospital gown again for a surgical revision. But when I finally get right back to the top of the timeline, I shed a tear as Jason signed off for the last time, thanking everyone for their support. He said that despite the years of pain and blow-out costs, the feeling of his dick lying against his thigh on a lazy Sunday afternoon made it all worthwhile.

My life thus became divided into two distinct parts. There was my daily waking life, where I worked and gave interviews about the importance of trans pride. Then there was my night-time waking life, where I obsessed over my dickless body and the likelihood of me ever being able to afford genital surgery. The price tag appeared to be north of $100,000, and the procedure was only performed by a single Australian surgeon, operating in Brisbane.

Brisbane. Meanjin. Not my neck of the woods. How could I possibly conjure up a need to fly to Brisbane, not to mention a six-figure bank balance?

In the witching hour, I began to search for more realistic alternatives. I developed a new expertise in packers: from ultra-realistic flaccid ones, made from the highest quality certified silicone, to lightweight foam inserts that was more akin to Ken's beige mound. You could select the packer that most closely matched your skin tone, whether stucco, cream, caramel or rich dark chocolate. If realism wasn't your thing, packers were also available in electric blue and midnight purple. It was even possible to choose between a circumcised and/an uncircumcised member.

Equal parts attracted and repulsed, I covertly ordered a mid-range, beige 'Mr Limpy' a week later. When my pale, contraband member arrived a few days later in discreet, plain packaging, I panicked. Was this really what I had been coveting? A wobbly little piece of skin and balls that looked like a turkey's neck? Both it and I were ridiculous. I shoved it in my sock drawer. But while I wasn't sure that I would ever want to wear one, my search for the ultimate packer continued.

One day, I spotted a petite crochet penis and testicles on Instagram, hand-stitched by a crafty bear called Brett. Each package was made-to-order, so I could choose everything from the shaft length to colour and testicle size. I could've even added ball hair.

Brett emailed to thank me for my order and told me my item would take him six to eight weeks to create. That was fine, I replied, it wasn't like I was going anywhere. I waited, occasionally giggling to myself about my penis's long-pending arrival. But three months later, no longer laughing, I contacted Australia Post, asking for an update on the whereabouts of my 'bespoke textile piece'.

After further delays, I was informed that it had been delivered to another flat in error. And that despite their best efforts, recovery had proved impossible. I tried to remind myself that it didn't matter; it wasn't exactly a life-or-death issue. But the fact that my hand-sewn little member was now sitting in somebody else's house, perhaps waiting to be gifted to a colleague in the annual Kris Kringle, made me feel ill. Perhaps I'd bought it as a joke, but that didn't mean just anyone had a right to laugh at it.

I contacted Brett to tell him what had happened. Devastated, he promised to make me a new one as soon as he'd got through his back orders. A month later, Brett and I met face to face outside my flat for hand delivery.

'Sorry it took so long. I was really just making these to take my mind off things, but this little business has really taken off,' said Brett.

He showed me some screenshots of his latest made-to-order creations: a small pink willy warmer with a rainbow thunderbolt, and a larger, tan-coloured uncircumcised member with bushy, brown testicles.

'I truly hope this gives you joy,' Brett said as he handed me mine, artfully wrapped in the *Star Observer*, Melbourne's gay street magazine.

Chapter 16
Big Rainbow

'They keep calling me Jeffrey Dahmer,' Terry said, my last client of the week.

I had no idea who that was.

'You know, the gay serial killer? From America?' Terry said.

I surreptitiously did a quick google search on my laptop as we spoke. There was a passing resemblance.

'Have you told your boss?' I asked.

'My boss is the one who started it,' he replied.

I took Terry through his options and agreed to help him lodge a discrimination complaint. When he left, I downloaded a true crime podcast about Jeffrey Dahmer and his wave of terror against the gay male community in Milwaukee in the 1980s. I put my headphones in and began listening to it on the tram on the way home, feeling a little guilty for indulging in such salacious, macabre entertainment.

The next day, we received some happy news. The Queer Legal Service had been nominated for a GLOBE award from Victoria's LGBTIQ business association. The email went on to explain that the rainbow sector's night of nights would be held at the Plaza Ballroom.

I called Polina to let her know. She was excited until she heard about the price tag for tickets.

'A table costs $1800? Sam, St Kilda Legal Service doesn't have that kind of money,' she said.

Just then, I received an incoming call from Gryn. 'I'd better see what he wants,' I told Polina, and hung up to speak to Gryn.

'Congratulations on the nomination,' he said.

He then told me that several of Pink Panther's services and health promotion initiatives had been nominated for awards in other categories, before offering me a seat at the Pink Panther table.

'If the Queer Legal Service wins, of course, we fully expect to come up and receive the award with you. I'll also need to review your speech,' he said.

Speech? I'd already scanned the awards website and seen that we were in direct competition with Rainbow Rights, so I was certain we weren't going to win.

'Gryn, I really haven't time to write a speech or anything. I was just going to wing it,' I said, glad for the opportunity to irritate him.

* * *

On the day of the awards ceremony, my single ticket allocation got bumped up to two at the last minute after someone else dropped out. Gemma got dressed in a flash and promised to meet me there. I hated fancy events like this, so was relieved that Gemma would be joining me. Hopefully she could charm Neil and Gryn, or at least help me ignore them. I'd realised late in the week that my suit no longer fitted me, so I had to make a last-minute dash to David Jones to buy a new one, effectively halving my fortnightly income.

As I walked down Swanston Street, I reflected on the extra space I was now permitted in public. When I was still read as female, I'd constantly have to move out of the way of men, lest a shoulder or stray elbow from a passing male hit me and sent me off balance. I don't think those men noticed that they were doing it, or that all women, young and old, were silently moving aside for them. My lesbian friends and I had created a game called the 'man-slam', where we'd refuse to get out of the way of men as a form of direct action. Whenever a man would run right into me, he'd look deeply confused by what had happened, as though my not moving for him was akin to a freak weather event. Now, even though at 5 foot 5 I was hardly imposing, women had started getting out of my way. Would this change in public status one day filter into my own sense of self? I wasn't sure.

When we arrived, we walked down the long winding staircase into a huge, castle-like ballroom with glittering golden chandeliers and sumptuous décor. I was relieved to see that for once a queer event was not rainbow-themed, but simply lit in a tasteful light-pink wash.

We were welcomed by deferential young waitstaff in tuxedos who offered Gemma and me champagne. I scanned the enormous room, trying to work out who everybody was, as my eyes adjusted to the dim lighting. To our left sat two tables of Helping Hands staff and volunteers, as well as a smattering of board members from Transgender Victoria. The Switchboard telephone counselling service staff were seated in the middle of the room, while our spots with Pink Panther were right at the front. Joy 94.9 were live broadcasting the event from a booth at the back of the room, breathlessly talking up the nominees. Gemma and I each accepted another champagne and went over to find Cassie at the Helping Hands table. They were all discussing some big gossip that had just dropped. Apparently, Neil and Gryn had upset the Pride Centre establishment committee at the last minute by pulling out of their long-standing plans to rent the entire top floor of the yet-to-be-built centre. This had suddenly left the Pride Centre without a main tenant, and people were wondering if it could survive the blow.

As Gemma and I drifted around the room, chatting with people I vaguely knew, it became increasingly clear to me that the entire LGBTIQ professional sector seemed to hate each other. Pink Panther and Helping Hands had apparently had a falling out over funding, as had the two big queer youth organisations. An intersex advocacy group weren't speaking with a trans support group because it had accepted a grant from a children's hospital that continued to perform irreversible cosmetic surgeries on intersex infants. Then, of course, there was Rainbow Rights, which I didn't much like. I watched Florence and her inner circle holding court at the front of the room, schmoozing with the LGBTIQ Commissioner and other senior government figures.

The lights went down, and we took our seats at the last possible moment. I was relieved to see that neither Gryn nor Neil was on my table, and that we'd been put with the AOD and family violence team. The big dogs were over on the next table, with the health promotion team.

A campy, young comedian who'd just got his own Netflix show appeared onstage in a pink-and-black suit.

'Welcome, ladies, gentlemen and they-friends to the twelfth annual GLOBE Awards!' he said, voice echoing throughout the building.

The acoustics in the venue were impressive, and quite unlike the humbler events I usually attended in the community legal sector. The comedian took us through the preliminaries, as the waitstaff brought entrées to the table and filled our wineglasses. The comedian asked for a moment of silence to acknowledge Bridget Flack, the young trans poet who'd died earlier that year. Groups huddled at the back, who had clearly not been listening, were angrily shooshed as the room fell into silence and the lights were dimmed. I didn't really want to think about Flack or the utterly tragic, and very public, end to her short life. So, I just stared at the huge, cascading curtains in the corners of the room, willing the moment to be over.

The lights came back, and the room broke out into applause as Frock Hudson, the drag queen from the Christmas picnic, took to the stage. This time she was dressed in a tight, iridescent dress with purple poms and an enormous curly sky-blue wig. Multiple squeals rang out across the ballroom as she began a live rendition of Sia's 'Chandelier'. It was actually pretty good. As my eyes followed Frock Hudson around the room, my gaze landed upon someone who seemed familiar yet very different. They were a tall redhead in an emerald-green dress. I felt like I'd seen them before, but where? My mind suddenly recognised who I was looking at. It was Dave. But Dave as I had never seen him, or her, before. It dawned on me that I'd made some very big assumptions about Dave that may not have been correct. I thought about going over to say hello, but I figured that they probably enjoyed clients coming up to them outside of work as much I did. So I just stayed put.

The event turned out to be just as boring as watching the Logies or the Brownlow, so I kept drinking to compensate. I drank so much, in fact, that I decided I wanted to have a cigarette, something I hadn't done in the better part of a decade. I asked Kiki, one of the AOD workers, who had a pack on the table if I could accompany her outside for a smoke.

We emerged from the cavernous ballroom back out onto a bustling Friday night on Collins Street, and found a small group of smokers in self-exile. Kiki introduced me around as she lit me a cigarette.

'Sam, this is Brienna, the head of the Pride Centre establishment committee.'

I smiled and shook her hand, as I inhaled the cigarette smoke. It tasted foul, like licking a burning newspaper. 'I've been meaning to come and speak to you,' I said, having another drag. 'I just heard about Pink Panther changing their plans,' I said.

Brienna's face dropped. 'Do you work with them too?' she asked.

'No – well, yes. Sort of? We are running a health justice partnership there, but we are an independent legal service. Anyway, we'd love to talk about renting a space at the Pride Centre when it opens,' I said.

'Have you spoken to Florence?' Brienna asked.

I was confused by the question. Why would I talk to Rainbow Rights about renting desk space at the Pride Centre?

I shook my head.

'Well, they've already approached us about running a queer legal service at the Pride Centre. They're in funding talks with the Fairer Victoria branch at the moment,' Brienna said.

It took me a moment to follow what she was saying. Could Rainbow Rights really be planning on launching their own queer legal service, less than a kilometre away from our office? I took another drag of my Marlboro, suddenly grateful for the acrid smoke. It wasn't like the government was going to fund two separate queer legal services. This was a declaration of war.

'Wow. No, I did not know that. I'll have to have a chat with them,' I replied, with a forced grin.

'Sorry. I assumed you knew. Neil knows. Pink Panther have been very supportive of their proposal, actually,' Brienna said.

Someone then came up to Brienna to introduce themselves, and I wandered off in a daze back to Kiki, who was giggling with a trio wearing skirts with pants and matching neon-lime wigs. They invited me to join them for a line in the bathroom, but I politely declined. I wasn't in the mood to stick around a second longer than I had to.

I returned to the ballroom just in time for my meal, a rubbery and flavourless chicken dish. I kept drinking. Gemma was having a great time chatting and laughing with the Pink Panther counsellors. I pretended to listen while stewing over the news. I suddenly remembered the award we'd been nominated for, the award that Rainbow Rights was sure to receive. I couldn't believe I would have to sit through Florence's inevitable acceptance speech in her posh, clipped voice.

The comedian retuned to the stage.

'Friends, it's now time to present the award for community advocacy.'

I suddenly felt Gryn's eyes on me from the next table. I ignored him and drained my glass. The comedian announced the nominees: Rainbow Rights, the Queer Legal Service and Switchboard, who'd recently spearheaded a campaign to include sexual orientation and gender identity in the national census.

'And the winner is ... Rainbow Rights!' the comedian said, as the room filled with applause.

I sat with the most neutral expression on my face that I could muster. Florence delivered her acceptance speech with all the flowery, vacant words of a career politician.

I decided to leave in the next break. I was sick to death of the rainbow industrial complex. I didn't want to ruin Gemma's night by telling her what I'd found out, so I just said I was tired and encouraged her to stay. Gemma, thoroughly ensconced in a hilarious conversation, stayed put and I left on my own.

As I waited for a rideshare, a group of guys piled out of another car.

'Is that Harry fucking Potter?' one of them said, pointing at me.

The men all cracked up. I turned my head away from them so they couldn't see my scowl. I knew they were just drunk, and probably had absolutely no idea that J.K. Rowling was, in addition to being one of the world's most successful writers, the world's most prominent TERF.

The next day, I contacted the Inclusive Victoria branch. I didn't know exactly who I was meant to speak to, and spent the day getting palmed off onto different people. Each senior bureaucrat said they hadn't heard anything about funding for a queer legal service at the Pride Centre. I was starting to wonder if I'd made the whole encounter with Brienna up when a branch director called Gabby called me back. I asked Gabby outright whether they'd offered funding to Rainbow Rights to set up a competing queer legal service.

'Absolutely not. We talk to a range of stakeholders about community priorities. We'd be more than happy to hear about the work you have been doing as well,' she said.

'Well, are you aware that St Kilda Legal Service already runs a queer legal service?' I asked.

'Yes, but we'd been told it was a relatively small operation,' she said.

'It's actually a state-wide service,' I said.

'Well, that's wonderful. We should add you, then, to the list of stake-holders to be contacted for the Pride Centre Legal Service scoping study. I'll just have to check to make sure it's not too late,' Gabby said.

'What scoping study?' I replied.

'Well, it's an initiative to try to map out the unmet legal needs of the LGBTIQ community, so that we can design a service that best meets those needs,' Gabby said.

'But we already run that service,' I replied.

'Exactly. That's why I'll try to add you to the stakeholder list,' she said.

* * *

Thus began the most frustrating and demoralising part of my job, where I had to attend countless meetings with Florence and seemingly clueless members of the Victorian public service, as Rainbow Rights undermined the new legal service I'd worked so hard to create.

Meanwhile, my caseload was as high as ever. I started to leave work later and later, and I was less inclined to go for a walk during my lunch break. I'd stopped talking to the AOD workers at Pink Panther because I was too busy, but I also didn't want them to see how unhappy I'd become. I wore my headphones all day and listened to background jazz songs to drown out the sounds of my colleagues. They were all so nice. Too nice. I had no time to talk. I had too much work to do.

Despite being well over capacity, I struggled to say no to new referrals. Every new client seemed to reveal a whole other area that society was failing in, or, rather, in which I myself was failing. One morning I conducted an intake session with a new client on the telephone. I went through my usual script.

'Name?'

'Tipene Smith.'

'Date of birth?'

'18 May 1993.'

'And how do you identity your gender?'

'Takatāpui.'

'Sorry, could you repeat that?'

'Takatāpui.'

I had no idea what Takatāpui meant, but also felt implicitly that this was something I should already know. I spelt it out on my intake form as best as I could, searching for the term online when I finished the call.

I soon learnt that Takatāpui was a traditional Māori term meaning 'intimate companion of the same sex'. It seemed that it had been reclaimed to embrace all Māori who identify as gay, lesbian, bisexual, intersex, non-binary or transgender. This term was not an option on my recently designed service intake forms, which included:

- man
- woman
- non-binary
- trans masculine
- trans feminine

I could see that I probably needed to learn from this experience and quickly decolonise my intake forms. But I also didn't want to stuff up my data, so I ticked non-binary and promised myself I'd do better with the forms when we got to the end of the pilot.

My last case that day was a referral from a youth organisation for a non-binary eighteen-year-old who'd received a rejection letter from Births, Deaths and Marriages Victoria after attempting to change their name to Bog Witch and their sex marker to 'nebulose'. When I first read the referral, I thought it was one of my friends having me on. But it turned out, Bog Witch was real.

I tried calling Bog but the call rang out and went to voicemail. A youthful, feminine recorded voice said, 'Hi, I never check this so please don't leave a message.' I hung up and sent Bog a text asking them to call me back.

They didn't feel comfortable meeting me in person, so we eventually agreed on a video call. A gothy-looking person with wispy blonde hair and a round baby-face stared back at me.

'Hi, Bog, it's Sam here from the Queer Legal Service. How are you?'
I began.

'It's Bog Witch,' they replied.

'Oh, sorry, I thought it was like a first name and a surname,' I said.

I'd always felt like I was terrible at building rapport with young people, and things didn't seem to be going well even with a member of my own community.

Bog Witch didn't want to send me their rejection letter from Births, Deaths and Marriages by email, so I asked them to hold it up to the screen. After a minute of failed attempts, I managed to make out that the registry had decided that Bog Witch was a prohibited name on the grounds that it was obscene or offensive.

While mulling over that, I looked up the definition of bog witch. There wasn't a lot of reputable sources available, but I found this description on a website called DeviantArt.

'Bog witches live solitary lives or in parasitic covens. While not secluded to Bogs as their name would suggest, Bog Witches prefer moist soils to build their living body hutches with. The term Witch is gender neutral, and both male and female Bog witches exist; though it is difficult to tell them apart.'

I certainly thought Bog Witch was a ludicrous and likely career-limiting name, but I didn't see how it was obscene. It did occur to me that even if Bog Witch had an arguable case, it nonetheless might not be in the interest of the Queer Legal Service for me to take it on. Was this really what the Stonewall rioters and the 78ers had been fighting for? I could just imagine the scandalous news headline if the *Herald Sun* found out.

'Do you think you could be happy with a different name?' I asked Bog Witch.

They shook their head. 'No. My real name is Bog Witch.'

'What about "non-binary" as your sex marker? You're definitely allowed that now,' I said.

'No. My gender is nebulose.'

I thought about it. Even though this case was a bit ridiculous, who was I to say what was important? Would it be lateral violence for me not to help, just because I thought their name was silly? I wasn't sure. To be on the safe side, I agreed to help Bog Witch.

Chapter 17
Trans Day of Additional Obligations

It was spring, and we were two months away from running out of funding. The scoping study had turned into an internal government pitch for budget funding. This forty-page document now had to pass through a series of byzantine bureaucratic processes before it could ever have the chance of transforming into actual, real money for a legal service, irrespective of who would actually be in charge of it. The Queer Legal Service, my proudest creation, had become my greatest nightmare, wreaking havoc upon my life and my increasingly unsteady mind.

Still worse, it was coming up to Trans Day of Visibility. I'd agreed to give a speech on the day at the Collingwood Neighbourhood Justice Centre, back when I was chirpy and enthusiastic. The Neighbourhood Justice Centre was an attempt to create a more hospitable court experience, where clients could receive support from social workers, AOD workers and housing services. It'd also launched a dedicated family violence list for the LGBTIQ community, so were keen to hear about how they could be more inclusive of trans clients.

Unfortunately, if there was one thing I categorically did not want to talk about anymore, it was me being transgender. My greatest joy was to go to a bar where no one knew me and order a drink as a regular, run-of-the-mill male. It's not that I especially loved getting called 'mate' in that particular way that Australian men speak to each other – I just didn't want to deal with being visibly gender non-conforming anymore. It was easier to hide out behind my new mask of manhood. But, alas, if I wanted any chance of securing the funding for the legal service, I felt like I couldn't be flaky. So off I went to roll myself out for a bunch of judges and court registrars and perform the 'trans lawyer' curiosity show.

I had a script by now which I could recite off the top of my head. 'We all want a fairer justice system that meets the needs of our diverse community. Just a few little steps – like providing gender-neutral toilets, offering additional options on forms and not assuming people's pronouns – can go a long way to make a trans or gender-diverse person feel more accepted by the justice system.'

It's not that I didn't believe it; I was just sick of saying it. But these trans inclusion days kept rolling around. There was International Day Against Homophobia, Transphobia and Biphobia, Trans Day of Visibility, Non-Binary People's Day, Trans Awareness Week and Trans Day of Remembrance, not to mention a cascade of inclusive events for Midsumma and Mardi Gras. In a better-funded organisation, we could quite legitimately hire a comms person to take on the role of appropriately acknowledging each other at these events. Why couldn't I just be left to my private gender misery, without the additional burden of having to pretend that I was feeling 'trans joy' and 'gender euphoria' at these events as well?

But I'd hitched my employment to my identity, and now I was paying the price. I was fed up to the back teeth of discussing gonads, genotypes, genitals, hormones and secondary anatomical features. But it seemed this was an inevitable consequence of having a job that I'd at least once found meaningful.

So, I was in a foul mood as I hurried down Johnston Street in time for the event. It was in a big brown brick building that had once housed a boot-making school. The foyer, with its recycled ironbark seating, was more reminiscent of a modern open-plan library than a court building. As soon as I saw the groups of staff waiting to hear me talk, I plastered a smile on my face and got ready to speak.

I sat down and listened to a speech by a red-headed trans man called Arnold, who'd been supporting trans clients on parole through Transgender Victoria since the early 2000s. Arnold was thoroughly burnt out now, he said, and was about to move in with his elderly mother in the country to get away from it all. Then it was my turn. Since Arnold had already taken the social space of burnt-out trans activist, with decades more service on the board than I had, I tried to appear as earnest and heartfelt as possible. I spoke about the invisible trans clients I represented in my role – people in prison, in immigration detention and in psychiatric wards. I said that they shouldn't look at me, a white trans lawyer, as a sign that real progress was being made, but that we still had far to go to support the most vulnerable and least socially palatable parts of our community with dignity and respect.

To my surprise, I received a standing ovation, and Arnold gave me a friendly shoulder squeeze. I was then able to decompress a little as Amao Leota Lu performed a touching, graceful traditional Samoan dance to round out the proceedings.

I was proud of us. But soon as it was over, I exited onto Wellington Street and let my expression drop back into a grimace.

When I arrived at my desk at Pink Panther, I received the news by email that Births, Deaths and Marriages had reversed their decision. It was official: there was now at least one Bog Witch in Melbourne with a legally nebulose sex.

* * *

Polina made an appointment with the chief adviser to the minister for fairness in an effort to address our funding woes. Polina thought that the minister might offer us some bridging funding to keep the Queer Legal Service going while we waited on the budget outcome. The chief adviser, Becky, had cancelled on us twice already at short notice, but today was the day we would finally speak. The boardroom in which I'd had my job interview was unavailable, so we crammed into a tiny meeting room in the corner of the building off from the front reception area. Our meeting was repeatedly interrupted by the frustrated remarks of clients waiting to receive meal relief boxes or nappies.

Becky wore a bright red lipstick, a neon-pink polka-dot blouse and a teal jacket. She looked like she'd be more comfortable launching a blockbuster exhibition at the NGV than crammed into the back office of a dingy little community centre. But she politely listened as I explained about the Queer Legal Service. She then asked me to talk a bit about my own story.

'You've got such a strong narrative here,' Becky said, when I had finished.

'About the legal service?' Polina asked.

'No, about Sam,' Becky said, looking at me with a beaming smile. 'Victoria's first transgender lawyer, bravely fighting the good fight, now needs some support themselves to stay afloat. "Save Our Sam" – I can see that printed on t-shirts. You could create a great GoFundMe for this.'

'I'm definitely not the first transgender lawyer. And we were sort of hoping that the minister could help us out,' I said.

'Well, I can only offer you advice. And my advice would be to create a compelling story that your community can really get behind. That way, there can be a bit of pressure behind your request, you see?' she said.

As soon as Becky left, I said to Polina, 'I'm not fucking doing that.'

'Well, it was disappointing they couldn't offer us any funding. But perhaps we should think about what she said,' Polina told me.

'No. I'm not being rolled out as a sob story. I don't want to be trans Bambi. I'd prefer to just walk away at this point,' I said.

'Well, obviously I can't stop you from leaving, Sam, but it would be terrible timing. Can you just wait and see what happens with the budget bid?' Polina asked.

I went to the kitchen and made myself a cup of tea. As I tipped the carton, spoiled, sour milk plopped into my drink. I sighed and chucked it down the sink. I missed Sandie.

On the train on the way home, I put my head in my hands. I felt that I both couldn't survive another moment in this job and that I must. I began to hope that we wouldn't be re-funded after all.

* * *

Polina booked all of the St Kilda Legal Service staff in for our annual training session about vicarious trauma, held at a large city law firm. The session was in acknowledgement of the well-established fact that lawyers are more susceptible to depression and anxiety than other parts of the community. The issue was being rehashed in the media that year after a local magistrate had tragically taken his life. They said that it had been due in part to the stress of a crippling workload. He had died just one week after attending a workplace wellbeing training session just like the one I was at, which made it feel pointless and grim.

Within the first five minutes of the session, I realised that my last two years could be a case study in what not to do to prevent vicarious trauma. I'd made every single mistake possible, and even come up with some new ones. It was quite clear to me before, during and after this training session that I was on a one-way trip to burnout. I'd spoken to a counsellor about it, and on weekends I regularly made bleak jokes about my state of mind to my friends. By that point I felt that there was little I could do, however, since I had opened many client files and agreed to do various things for various people. I didn't have the emotional reserves to deal with the stress of telling my clients I couldn't help them in the next stage of their case, and that they'd have to go it alone from here. I knew that it would be much harder to convince similarly time-poor lawyers at other centres to help me out by taking on a case or two, than it would be to just knuckle down and do all the work myself. Not only that, I also felt that my personal reputation was on the line since I'd done so much media to promote the service. I wanted to show my community and others that trans people could excel at anything they chose, and that we were just as employable as anyone else. I was loathe to be seen as unreliable.

At the end of the session, the trainer told us to write three things on a postcard that we were going to do to look after ourselves. I dutifully wrote down, *Go to the gym, drink less and start reading novels again.* She then collected our postcards and told us that she'd mail them out a month later. Mine never arrived.

* * *

One morning, I woke up to the news that a former AFL player and coach had been arrested for stalking and breaching a family violence order. An officer at St Kilda Police Station had taken an unauthorised photograph of the former player wearing a platinum blonde wig, heavy make-up and a black dress, and then leaked it to other officers via WhatsApp. That image, along with a mugshot, soon ended up in the hands of the media, which chose to splash the images across Australia. While locked up in the mental health unit of a Melbourne remand centre, Danielle Laidley was outed as trans to the entire nation.

Danielle Laidley had grown up in Balga, a working-class suburb in northern Perth, just down the road from where I was raised. She'd played half-back for the West Coast Eagles in the early 1990s, so my brother and I had cheered her on in our early days in Australia.

I called Polina. 'This happened right on our doorstep. I really think the Queer Legal Service has to put out a press release calling for the police officers to be stood down and investigated.'

Polina agreed. By 9.30 a.m. our statement that the release of the photos was a shocking breach of privacy which would further damage the relationship between the police and the rainbow community had been picked up by newspapers across Australia.

This made Neil from Pink Panther very, very angry. Gryn was instructed to pass the message along to Polina and me.

'How dare you make comments like this without running them past us?' he snapped down the phone line. 'Comments which we would have never agreed to, I might add. We value our relationship with the Victorian government far too much to be saying inflammatory things like this.'

It seemed that we had a major misunderstanding about who was allowed to say what and when.

I said to Polina, 'Well, we are an independent organisation, so they can't tell us what to do.'

'They seem to think that they co-own the Queer Legal Service branding and that everything we say has to go via them first,' said Polina.

This was news to me. I looked back through the memorandum of understanding we'd signed when I'd first started. There was nothing about who owned what. It appeared that our two organisations had very different ideas about what was going on here. Issues that we could have probably nutted out if they'd regularly attended our monthly steering committee meetings.

I would have loved nothing more than to avoid Pink Panther for a while, but I had two client appointments booked there that afternoon. So, I made my way over to Flinders Street Station and caught a tram down St Kilda Road, desperately hoping I wouldn't bump into Neil or Gryn in the lifts.

My last client of the day was Kassandra, a queer woman from Reservoir. I'd helped Kassandra a few times before with an ongoing tenancy issue in her community housing property. But when she arrived, she told me she didn't want help with that anymore and just wanted me to register a new business name for her. I paused before answering.

'Kassandra, this is not the kind of thing community legal centres assist with. I'm afraid I'm not going to be able to help you with your business registration,' I said.

I didn't know what would happen next, but I was sure it wouldn't be good.

'How could you abandon me like this?' Kassandra said, before bursting into tears.

I offered her a tissue, and waited while she gathered up her things.

'You pretend to be nice, but then you just turn your back on people. I'm going to let everyone know who you really are, Sam,' she said, as she stormed out of the interview room.

Again, the spectre of being called out by a member of the community online reared its head. I wrote an extensive file note explaining exactly what had happened, and why I'd made the decision not to help her.

A few hours later, Kassandra sent me graphic images of her bloody, cut-up arms. There was no text attached, but there didn't need to be. I felt frightened and incredibly angry. I did my best to push down my ugly feelings, and followed our workplace protocol by calling the Crisis Assessment and Triage Team. While I listened to the on-hold music, I felt sick about having to hold to my ear the mobile phone that held the disturbing photos.

After a few minutes, the muzak abruptly ended and a friendly man with a jolly northern British accent introduced himself and started to ask me questions in a breezy manner.

'How deep did the cuts look?'

'Um, I'm not sure, I only looked at them for a second and then called you,' I replied.

'Fair enough, fair enough. Well, if you wouldn't mind having a wee look for me again, just to check?' he asked.

I put my phone on speaker and looked at the messages.

'Not that deep. Sorry, I got scared because of all the blood.'

'That's fair! Well, I don't think we'll need to send someone over immediately, then, but do you mind if I call her?' he asked cheerfully.

'Not at all' I replied, immensely relieved that he was now taking over responsibility for the situation.

He called me back twenty minutes later to let me know that he'd spoken to her and her friend who'd just arrived, and she was feeling safe and supported. I sighed when I hung up, and took myself out for lunch. Halfway through my bagel I received a call from Kassandra's friend, who yelled at me for getting the state involved and for not understanding the difference between a genuine suicide attempt and a standard cry for help.

* * *

As we continued to await the budget outcome, I kept working on writing the inclusive practice toolkit for community lawyers, the last piece of the puzzle before I could acquit the pilot funding grant. Polina and I were beginning to plan a launch event for the toolkit at St Kilda Town Hall when the location of the annual Community Legal Centre conference was announced one afternoon. It was to be in Brisbane. Meanjin. Home of the Brisbane Lions, XXXX beer, and the only surgeon who performs phalloplasties in Australia. Of course I would launch the toolkit up there, in the last week of my job before the funding ran out. It seemed like fate.

Chapter 18
Just Passing Through

I was still trapped in the suffocating cycle of work-related anxiety, exhaustion and fear when Gemma and I head to Melbourne Airport. Since I was also nervous about going through airport security and paranoid about flight times, I was almost completely unhinged by the time we arrived. Having previously experienced my bizarre behaviour to and from the airport, Gemma did her best to keep things cheerful, cracking jokes along the way.

This time, my anxiety homed in on the security body scanners. After checking our luggage, I pre-emptively took off my belt, shoes and jacket and hung them off my backpack, which did little to help me appear cool, calm and collected as we approached airport security. After pushing my carry-on luggage through the conveyer belt, I approached the white tube-like scanning station. I'd been too scared to wear my crochet packer, but now I was wondering if that too had been a mistake. How on earth could I get through this X-ray machine without attracting undue attention on my discordant body?

'Arms up, feet on the mat, thanks,' a bored-looking security guard said.

I held my arms up like Jesus nailed to the cross as the machine whirred around me. If I had to be patted down for concealed weapons, would they choose a male or a female security guard? What if the machine got confused and started beeping? Would I be taken to a tiny room and strip searched, while airport staff stared and laughed at my mismatched upper and lower halves?

'You're fine, come through,' the security guard said.

As I walked past, I spotted a generic cartoon outline of myself on the guards' monitor, with the word FEMALE flashing underneath. I felt inordinately distressed by the word.

As we collected our bags, I sighed. I would never ever be free of being transgender. I knew it in my hip bones.

Gemma and I then browsed the airport bookshop, returning to passing as an ordinary heterosexual couple on our way to Queensland. Brexit was all over the newspapers, having finally been enacted in the UK. At least I wouldn't have to go to the trouble of updating my gender on my UK passport now. It hardly seemed worth it since I'd lost the right to live in continental Europe.

We stopped in for a drink at Movida. As usual, when our drinks came out, we had to swap them as they were being served. It seemed that no one could quite believe that a man would ever order himself a glass of rosé.

We eventually shuffled our way onto the plane and listened as an air hostess sagely advised applying one's own oxygen mask before attempting to assist others. As I browsed the menu in the airline magazine, I caught myself wondering which meal and drink combo would make me appear the most masculine. Peanuts and beer? Pringles and a whisky? Definitely not the salad and a white wine, which is what I actually wanted.

* * *

I'd booked us into an art deco Airbnb in Highgate Hill. I'd never heard of the suburb, but it was close enough to the Avid Reader bookshop, my only cultural marker for Brisbane.

Before booking, I'd scrolled through my Airbnb reviews to confirm that I was still considered a good guest. I noticed that the old reviews had 'she' and 'her' in them, so I contacted Airbnb to update my gender information, as I thought it might be confusing for hosts when my new masculine form showed up to take the keys. Airbnb replied that they'd changed me to an M, but that their policy specifically prevented them from altering my prior hosts' use of pronouns in my reviews. They'd come up with a nifty workaround, however, which was that they could change my pronoun to '[GUEST]'. So, my updated review from Maria in Eaglehawk Neck, for example, now stated, 'Sam is a wonderful guest and we were happy to have [GUEST'S] partner arrive for [GUEST'S] second night (by arrangement).' Linda from Hobart was equally effusive: 'Sam was a pleasure to host. [GUEST] was respectful of the rules and left it clean and tidy. I wouldn't hesitate to recommend [GUEST] to other hosts.'

The next morning, Gemma and I got on a pair of rental e-scooters, which were being trialled across Brisbane, and headed for the Sofitel Hotel, the wind in our hair. From there, Gemma went off to meet up with friends, while I headed upstairs to the conference. I grabbed my name tag, conference lanyard and customary tote bag filled with pens and flyers, and plonked myself down in a corner to write my presentation. The first sessions of the day were 'Activate: The Power of Community Legal Centres to Defend Activist Spaces' and 'Deep Impact: Social Impact of Natural Disaster and Organisational Responses to Environmental Issues'. Both sounded right up my alley, but I was so stretched that the thought of attending any of the very interesting conference sessions seemed a remote possibility.

At around eleven a.m., as people began streaming out of the first session, my spidey senses started tingling. God, there was Florence and her entourage. I didn't think they'd be here. I tried to ignore them and went back to my presentation.

When it was time for my session, I saw a small crowd amassing in the lobby. I couldn't believe it – Florence had organised an 'emergency breakout session' about the Religious Discrimination Bill outside the official conference schedule, at the exact time I was presenting 'Purposeful Inclusion: Working with LGBTIQ+ Communities'. Rainbow Rights were even handing out bags, t-shirts and promotional stickers to build interest. If they'd been so desperate to present at this conference, why didn't they pitch to run a session like the rest of us? Or had they come up to Queensland specifically to annoy me as much as humanly possible?

I entered the large conference room and loaded my presentation onto the giant screen, wondering whether anybody would even come, given Rainbow Rights' impromptu session right outside the door. Dribs and drabs of my colleagues from across Australia trickled in, and by the time I was due to kick off there was a respectable crowd. I stood at the head of the room and began discussing all the topics I was deeply sick of: pronouns, gender-neutral toilets, data collection and the importance of celebrating key LGBTIQ days in the workplace. Despite my feelings, I was able to put on a good show of enthusiasm, and everyone promised to implement my suggestions in their own workplaces.

When it was over, I took myself off to the toilet to decompress for a while. It suddenly occurred to me that I had, as of that moment, scaled the mountain and achieved all the goals laid out in our original grant application.

- Deliver LGBTIQ practice toolkit – tick

- Provide five professional legal education sessions – tick

- Deliver 500 legal advices, 150 minor work files and 50 cases – tick

- Write a final report addressing unmet legal needs in the LGBTIQ community – tick

Tick, tick, tick. I had done it. Sadly, I didn't feel the sense of accomplishment that I had hoped for. I just felt tired and sweaty.

* * *

That afternoon, I managed to catch a session called 'Prisons and Policing: Dismantling Unjust Systems and Practices', before heading off on an e-scooter to see the surgeon. I hadn't bothered to make an appointment. I didn't even have enough money for the first of the three procedures, which would be a hysterectomy. I thought it would be fun to go down there anyway, though, to see what it would feel like to be at the place that could make my dreams come true. It was an idyllic Brisbane day. The trees in the City Botanic Gardens glittered as I flew past them then over the bridge towards the Maritime Museum. I hung a right and sped past the Gabba before going into East Brisbane, which I'd never been to before. My route then took me along Norman Creek and a beautiful, expansive bikeway through glorious parklands. I began to lose enthusiasm for my strange adventure when the map took me down the side of a busy freeway. By the time I arrived at the medical centre, I'd decided that this time, I'd really lost my mind. What was I doing there? Who went on tours of generic private hospitals in the suburbs, just to fantasise about a prohibitively expensive gender-affirming medical procedure?

I entered a pharmacy and bought a bottle of Evian water to soothe my parched throat. That would have to do as my holiday souvenir. I lined up at the cab rank full of sore, tender patients, and asked the driver to take me back to the conference.

When I returned, the conference afterparty had descended into a daggy disco. The DJ was playing Sophie Ellis-Bextor's 'Murder on the Dancefloor', presumably at the behest of one of the criminal lawyers as a joke. I found some fellow Victorians I vaguely knew and had a drink with them, and then kept drinking some more. I loved community lawyers. Around them, I never felt like a square peg in a round hole.

When things began to wrap up, I hired another e-scooter and rode back across the Kurilpa Bridge and down Riverside Drive. I was joyously, recklessly drunk, and certain that I'd never travel by any other mode again. I caught up with Gemma and her friends at a bar. I tried not to think about what my last two years of hard work had all meant, and whether my efforts to build something lasting would be wiped out by a stroke of a pen from a government expenditure review committee.

* * *

The next day, Gemma and I borrowed a friend's ute and drove north towards Noosa, where we'd booked a room for the night to celebrate the end of my project. As usual, Gemma drove and I sat happily in the passenger seat, choosing the music and offering refreshments. Along the way we stopped at Golden Beach, a long, thin, sheltered spit of sand on the Sunshine Coast. It was time for my first swim post-surgery. As I took off my shirt, revealing my bare flesh at the beach for the first time, I felt deeply self-conscious. My mind conducted yet another unwanted assessment of my body. Feet: too small. Belly: too large, with a sad, frowning belly button which, post-transition, now seemed to always have dark lint caught in it. On the upside, my shoulders were broader and my thicker neck was ringed with curls, which had begun to emerge when I decided to stop cutting my hair altogether.

I was worried that my too-large hips and the shiny pink scars across my chest would give me away. But as I looked around, no one looked back at me. A bearded man in red board shorts was supervising a toddler, who was happily splashing around in the shallows. An older couple with deeply tanned leathered skin read magazines on towels laid out across the glistening sand. None of them seemed to care about my slightly unusual body.

* * *

On the plane on the way home, a man sat behind me with his rowdy three-year-old son.

'Rex, don't kick the seat, my love, the man in front of you might not like that,' he said.

The boy stopped kicking, and there was a brief pause.

'Daddy, is that man a boy or a girl?'

My heart stopped. I didn't want to know what would happen next.

'Does it matter?' the father replied.

'I guess not,' replied the child.

Epilogue

We didn't get the funding. However, neither did Rainbow Rights. At the eleventh hour, Helping Hands teamed up with another community legal centre and swooped in to secure the money to run a 'brand-new' queer legal service.

I got another community law job, assisting international students with wage theft and sexual harassment claims. I lasted twelve weeks before having to admit defeat. I was burnt out, and I didn't know when or even if I'd be able to practise law again.

Gemma's legal career, on the other hand, was going from strength to strength. She'd been promoted at Legal Aid and was studying for the bar exam. While Gemma's notes took up every available bit of wall space as she tried to cram more legal knowledge into her head than ever, I tried my best to move on from Lady Justice.

We said goodbye to Sissie, Enid, Moxie and Bobo, and moved into a tiny flat in Seddon above a coffee shop. We said we'd catch up, but I didn't think we ever really would. The new place had sealed windows and reverse-cycle air conditioning. It didn't have a lift, however, so I had to lug Tibby's increasingly arthritic body up and down the stairs three times a day, which soon replaced the gym as my main form of exercise. I went to my local GP to get back on a mental healthcare plan. After explaining my situation, my doctor asked me if she should put 'being transgender' under the reason for a referral. I said no. When she handed me the printed-out plan, I saw that I'd been listed as female. I politely asked for the document to be amended. She took the mental healthcare plan off me, crossed out female with a pen and handwrote male in its place. As I walked home, I tried hard to see the humour in it all.

When the pandemic hit, I got lucky and landed a temporary job at a local council. Financially, my dreams of further gender-affirming surgery remained as far away as ever, but at least I was sleeping again.

I kept myself occupied by reading, exploring my surrounding streets, and watching the Tokyo Olympics. There, I found a new trans sporting icon in Laurel Hubbard, a forty-three-year-old women's weightlifter from New Zealand. Her inclusion in the women's competition created controversy, with some arguing that she had an inherent biological advantage by having been through male puberty. A large media contingent thus followed Hubbard to all her events. Despite having been deemed a strong medal contender by the media, she failed to complete her three snatch lifts and was eliminated in the first round. I listened to her post-Games interview. She was sweet, shy, considered and, above all, magnanimous in defeat. 'Although I haven't really achieved the results I and others had hoped for, I'll be able to leave with a pocketful of memories of extraordinary moments. That will be as rewarding as any Olympic medal could be.'

I hoped to one day feel such gratitude.

* * *

It's now been three years since I quit working in the law.

I miss it every day.

My world feels much smaller without all the clients I used to meet. I miss the minor victories that we achieved together, and the sense of perspective their struggles gave me. I feel nostalgic for the falling-down, brown brick building in St Kilda, now that I'm working in a gigantic, glass office tower in the city. I even miss the old server in the toilet.

I am read as male almost all the time now, which comes with a range of benefits. More people listen to me when I'm speaking and don't bump into me as I walk down the street. I can buy the clothes I want without staff raising an eyebrow, and I'm getting better at setting boundaries. I'm still working on body acceptance. I'm scared by the likelihood of having to go into hospital again at some point. I feel anxious at the thought of my discordant, unclothed body being prodded and poked by horrified doctors and nurses. I worry about how I will be treated if I ever need to go into aged care.

Now and then, I try to tally up what we managed to achieve during the short life of the Queer Legal Service. The long-discussed Religious Discrimination Bill was nixed by moderate conservatives, and ScoMo got kicked out in the 2022 election. I'm not convinced the guy who replaced him as prime minister is big on transgender rights, but he did turn up to Mardi Gras. I don't know if my inclusive practice toolkit was ever implemented by any community legal centres, or if it's been consigned to history, like so many other 'exciting new resources'.

Sometimes, I love being part of the LGBTIQ community. Other times, I'm certain it's a fictional group made up by a few CEOs of not-for-profits to ask for funding, and that we're all just a disparate bunch of complicated people with many of the same enemies. But every time Midsumma rolls around, I keep on showing up.

We're now in the midst of a global transgender rights backlash, and it's hard to hard to know how things will end up. Will my life as a transgender lawyer specialising in queer law one day be seen as little more remarkable than a lesbian couple on a weekend away in Day-lesford? Or were these the Weimar years for the trans community, as good as they will ever be?

Acknowledgements

Firstly, thank you to my partner, Gemma Cafarella, for your love and support over the years. You bring the world together with your huge personality, love for life and passion for social justice. Special shout-out for unexpectedly parenting my teenage niece with me during a pandemic. It's difficult to express how grateful I am for everything you've done for both of us. Thanks to the whole Cafarella/Goodwin clan for the welcoming Ella and I into your family and for all the home-cooked meals.

Thanks to Terri-ann White from Upswell for believing in this book and to Rebecca Bauert for all the insightful feedback.

I have been incredibly well supported by numerous Australian arts and literary institutions for the many years I spent working on this book. I would have never completed it without your support and encouragement. Firstly, thanks to the Wheeler Centre for offering me the completely unexpected, transformative Next Chapter Fellowship during this queer legal saga, and to Chloe Hooper, my Next Chapter mentor throughout 2020, that most tumultuous year. Thanks to staff past and present at Varuna – The National Writers' House for providing a wonderfully generative place for writing and to the Scribe team for accepting me into their residency program. Many thanks to the Australian Society of Writers for awarding me with a Fellowship, and for pairing me with the astute Nadine Davidoff during that time. Thanks to Creative Victoria for providing me with a 2021 creative development grant and to the City of Melbourne for access to River Studios and for selecting me for a Boyd Garrett residency. Many thanks to Footscray Community Arts and the West Writers Group for the ongoing support and encouragement. Thanks also to

The Clocktower Centre, Moonee Ponds for providing me with access to their free emerging writers' room.

I am immensely grateful to the many literary journals and outlets that have published my work over the past few years, including *The Age, Antithesis Journal, Archer Magazine, ArtsHub, Australian Book Review, Baby Teeth Journal, Bent Street, The Big Issue, Bowen Street Press, Fruit Queer Literary Journal, Grattan Street Press, Griffith Review, Kill Your Darlings, The Long Lede Anthology, Mascara Literary Review, Meanjin, Overland, The Saturday Paper, Spineless Wonders, The Suburban Review, Sydney Review of Books, un Magazine, Vertigo, The Victorian Writer* and *Verandah Journal*. Special thanks to *Griffith Review* for publishing my essays 'The Sad Stats: The Trauma of Community Law' and 'Detachable Penis: Gender Dismembered', *Antithesis Journal* for publishing 'The Evidence', *The Suburban Review* for publishing 'Tops', *Mascara Literary Review* for publishing 'Elasticity', and to *Baby Teeth Journal* for publishing 'The Nub' and 'Passport Control', all of which have been partially reworked into this book.

I've done so many helpful writing courses over the years. Thanks to Varuna and George Haddad for running Queer Backyards and to Rick Morton for running their Light and Shade Masterclass. Thanks to Writers Victoria for always running fantastic classes, with a special mention to Ellena Savage and Sam Van Zweden for their Creative Non-Fiction classes, Writing the Body with Lee Kofman and Radical Memoir Writing with Lamisse Hamouda.

Thank you to Transgender Victoria for supporting Yves Rees and me to run the Spilling the T Collective for trans and gender-diverse writers as a peer support project, and to each and every writer who took part in that project. A big thanks also to Gordon Thompson from Clouds of Magellan Press who encouraged Yves and me to guest edit what became the final edition of *Bent Street: Soft Borders, Hard Edges*. Many thanks to my fellow *Nothing to Hide: Voices of Trans and Gender-Diverse Australia* co-editors – Alex Gallagher, Yves Rees and Bobuq Sayed – and all the contributors, and to Allen & Unwin for publishing the anthology. I learnt so much from being a part of producing both anthologies and am immensely grateful to everyone who played a part.

Thanks to my Carlton queer writers' group – Jonathan Butler, Savannah Hollis, Jack Nicholls, Jasper Peach and Yves Rees – your insights and support have been invaluable. Thanks also to Bad Writers Club and The Chestnut Tree, West Footscray for the Write Your Effing Heart Out sessions.

To my other great love, community radio. Thank you for supporting me and my many projects over the years and for welcoming me onto the airwaves. Thanks to Joy 94.9 for letting Gemma and me host Transgender Warriors and to all the amazing people we interviewed. Your collective wisdom kept me going in a difficult time. Thanks to 3CR's Done By Law crew for keeping the community law sector together with the great shows and boozy annual trivia nights. A million thanks to Triple R for having Gemma, Hamish McLachlan and me on to host Queer View Mirror, and for occasionally even letting me on Breakfasters! Thanks also to the ABC for commissioning Gemma, James Milsom and me to create 'Crossing Time: A History of Transgender Australia' for *The History Listen*.

Thank you to the many trans and gender-diverse trailblazers, writers and activists who continue to inspire me. Thanks to the Australian Queer Archives and all the historians who utilise it to preserve LGBTIQ history. Many thanks to all librarians everywhere. I must've written this book at half the libraries around Australia. Thank you for preserving a free, accessible place for people to read, write and learn wherever we are in this country.

Thank you to the many extraordinary community law colleagues I've had over the years. There are too many of you to name but special thanks must go to all the St Kilda Legal Service volunteers, as well as Annie Davis, Sam Drummond, Monique Hurley, Hannah Sycamore and Verena Tan for all the insightful chats about the sector over the years. Thanks to Community Legal Workers United/Australian

Services Union crew for continuing to campaign for workplace justice. Thanks also to my 2019 Centre for Australian Progress fellows for the important discussions and solidarity during the events of this book. To my dear friends Annie Hooper, Darcy O'Connell and Emma Torzillo, thanks for all the support and laughs over the many years. To the many counsellors I have had over the years, thank you so much for working with me and sorry for being weird and avoidant. It's me, not you!